DEALS WITH THE DEVIL

AND OTHER REASONS TO RIOT

DEALS

WITH THE

DEVIL

AND OTHER REASONS TO RIOT

PEARL CLEAGE

ONE WORLD

BALLANTINE BOOKS • NEW YORK

A One World Book
Published by Ballantine Books

Copyright © 1987, 1989, 1990, 1991, 1992, 1993 by Pearl Cleage

Some of the essays in this book were previously published in the *Atlanta
Tribune* and in *Mad at Miles: A Blackwoman's Guide to Truth*, published by
The Cleage Group, Inc., in 1990.

"In My Solitude" first appeared in *Essence* Magazine in February 1989 and
is reprinted here by permission.

"We Who Believe in Freedom" first appeared in *Why L.A. Happened*
edited by Haki Madhubuti, Third World Press, 1993.

Grateful acknowledgment is made to the following for permission to
reprint previously published material:
The Famous Music Publishing Companies: Excerpt from the lyrics of
"Solitude" by Eddie DeLange, Irving Mills, and Duke Ellington.
Copyright © 1934 by Mills Music, Scarsdale Music, and Famous Music.
Copyright © Renewed. Excerpt from the lyrics of "Love Shoulda Brought
You Home" by Daryl Simmons, Boaz Watson, and Kenneth B. Edmonds.
Copyright © 1992 by Ensign Music Corporation, Green Skirt Music, Saba
Seven Music, and Kear Music.

Simon & Schuster, Inc.: Excerpt from *Miles Davis: The Autobiography* by
Miles Davis with Quincy Troupe. Copyright © 1989 by Miles Davis.
Reprinted by permission of Simon & Schuster, Inc.

Library of Congress Catalog Card Number: 92-97479

ISBN: 0-345-38278-1

Designed by Ann Gold
Manufactured in the United States of America

First Edition: August 1993

10 9 8 7 6 5 4 3 2 1

FOR DEIGNAN

ACKNOWLEDGMENTS

I want to thank Zaron W. Burnett, Jr., my favorite Carthaginian, whose love and intelligence are all over these pages; my sistereditor Cheryl Woodruff for her faith and guidance; my family for their patience; and my friends for life Walter R. Huntley, Jr., Bill Bagwell and Mongo Lee for their understanding during the creation of this work. I also appreciate the continuing support of *The Atlanta Tribune,* Just US Theater Company, The Cleage Group, Inc. and Third World Press who previously have presented some of the work included in this book.

CONTENTS

CONTENTS

CONTENTS

DEALS WITH THE DEVIL:
BY WAY OF INTRODUCTION

I am not a religious person but I do believe in magic, mysteries and deals cut at the crossroads under the full moon (if the spell includes love sought or lost) or the new moon (if the spell centers on fame and fortune) or no moon at all if The Deal demands those particular bargains with the Devil that do not begin with love gone wrong or dreams deferred but with a weird desire to be something that stands alone, set apart from friends and family; cut off from community and comrades; solitary and singular; a bizarre solo act, singing its own back up to avoid even the semblance of group activity and grinning at the gates like just because The Deal was done in darkness, it will never come to light . . .

. . . Which, of course, it will. And it does. As regularly as rape and race riots and magic, in which I have already confessed a belief which I believe to be a semi-genetic predisposition resulting from my status as the youngest child of a charismatic preacher. I grew up watching my father talk passionately to God in public once a week. Deals with the Devil were at least as real as the intricate bargains with God that we, his chosen people, were required to make in our endless pursuit of salvation, especially after I finally got up the nerve to ask my father if he really believed in God.

"I believe in God and the Devil," he said calmly, "because I've had communication with them both."

At the time, I accepted this as fact, and I still do, although my image of the Devil sitting in my father's study debating some point of theology or politics has evolved into an understanding of the fact that while only those who have faith and patience get to talk to God, everybody gets to talk to the Devil. And if The Deal goes down like it's supposed to, some people get to talk for him. . . .

. . . Which would be okay if they all wore those red satin capes and carried three-pronged pitch forks so we'd know whose side they were on. But they don't. Disguise and camouflage are a big part of The Deal. That's why it's only done in darkness and why it's always so spooky when it finally leaps out into your headlights, drooling and dancing and demanding its propers before you go *anutha futha* because what goes around always comes around . . .

. . . In spades.

PART ONE

MAD

AT

MILES

WHY I WRITE

Yesterday, as I was writing this, my neighbor, my sister, had to call the police to protect her from her husband, also my neighbor and my brother, who was threatening to douse them both with gasoline and light it in a murder/suicide if she did not stop divorce proceedings and come back to be his wife.

Last week after class, one of my students waited for me to confess softly that her boyfriend had been beating her and what should she do?

A month ago, a young friend who teaches preschool read to me from her journals a harrowing description of the night her former lover shot himself in the head after she escaped from his apartment following months of beating and torture.

My friend the corporate executive relates a story of leaping from a speeding car and running into some urban woods after her husband placed a gun to her temple while driving with her down a busy suburban street.

My friend the well-respected public servant comes to work with sunglasses to hide the two black eyes her husband gave her by beating her head against the wall while their children slept in the next room.

My sisterwriter with the three young children tells horror stories of being scalded with boiled water and forced to suck the barrel of a gun as if it was her husband's penis.

And my memory of my own nightmare as an undergraduate student at Howard University, listening to my boyfriend tell me I'd better not move as he tied my hands and feet and told me if he couldn't have me, nobody could.

But that's not all. I also remember the chorus of black male objections to Ntozake Shange's *For Colored Girls*. I hear the protests over Alice Walker's *The Color Purple*, and I remember the forums whining about negative images of black men in *The Women of Brewster Place*, and I wonder where those same black male voices are when black male violence is being condoned and taught and glamorized and ignored. I wonder when we are going to see the same commitment to fighting sexism in the work of our brotherwriters that we see to fighting racism. I wonder how much good all those poems about beautiful African queens can do in the face of a backhand slap across the mouth and a merciless rape in the bedroom of your own house.

I wonder why Haki Madhubuti and Zaron Burnett, Jr., and Donald Stone are the exceptions and not the rule when their works focus on black male responsibility for admitting to and then stopping the war that is being waged against black women and children by the men who should be our closest allies and most ardent advocates.

But one thing I do not wonder about anymore is why I am writing and what concerns shape and focus my politics, my aesthetics, my form and my content. I remember exactly when it became clear to me.

It was my birthday. My forty-first birthday, to be exact. And it began like any other day with me stumbling out of bed to wake my daughter, wishing it wasn't still dark outside in the winter when you have to get up early and wondering what to fix for breakfast. The breakfast question led me into the kitchen where I flipped on the morning news to be sure my country had not invaded somebody while I was sleeping. That's when I heard it.

"A lone gunman, armed with an automatic weapon, opened fire on a group of female students in Montreal, killing fourteen and wounding thirteen others. The man, who apparently had a grudge against women, shouted, 'You're all feminists!' before firing point-blank into a group of female students."

The anchorwoman read the copy with the bland unconcern that is her trademark and then went on to tell me about the approach of a winter storm. But I didn't hear it. I was stunned. What kind of murderer was this? Was he angry enough at feminism to pick a random bunch of young women and shoot them down in cold blood? I was angry and frightened and confused.

When I got the morning paper, it didn't do much to reassure me. Photographs on the front page showed wounded women being carried out of the classroom building where they had been shot. Their friends huddled around in small, weeping groups, trying to understand and cope with their grief. A policeman called to the scene found his own daughter among the dead and dying. A male student who survived said, "I heard the gunman say, 'I want the women!' He separated us into two groups, the guys in one corner and the girls in another. When that was done, he asked the guys to leave and then he just started shooting."

I got through the rest of my morning routine, although I don't know how. My daughter shared my shock and horror at what had happened and although I saw the questions in her eyes, I didn't have the reassuring answers that mothers are always supposed to have, no matter what. I didn't have any way to explain to her what this kind of killing was about. I didn't even have a way to explain it to myself yet. It was just scary.

I spent the day looking for news about the gunman and hoping I wouldn't find it. I watched the television broadcasts, listened to the radio reports and made sure I got the afternoon paper for any updated information, but it didn't help me understand more or feel any better. Finally, I had to admit to myself that I wasn't really looking for any explanations. I was looking for a news bulletin that said it was all a mistake. That it had never happened. That a crazy man had not chosen as his target women he identified as feminists, whether they identified themselves that way or not.

By the end of the day, I had to admit that no bulletin was forthcoming. The facts and the death toll remained as grim as they had been when I first heard it on the morning news. The only question that remained was what I was going to do about it.

I was at a loss as to what the correct response should be. I am not a violent person. I own no weapons and have never been in a fight in my life. I am not an organizer and I have no troops to marshal with marching songs and battle plans. What I do is write about what I see and what I feel and what I know in the hope that it will help the people who read it see more and feel more and know more.

It was clear to me by nightfall that the only question I had to answer in the face of the act of war committed against women in Montreal was why I am writing. So I said a prayer for my fallen sisters and for the five women who are murdered in America every day by their husbands or ex-husbands or boyfriends and tried to answer the question as honestly as I could so I wouldn't forget it when there were no headlines or front-page horror stories to remind me.

I am writing to expose and explore the point where racism and sexism meet. I am writing to help myself understand the full effects of being black and female in a culture that is both racist and sexist. I am writing to try and communicate that information to my sisters first and then to any brothers of goodwill and honest intent who will take the time to listen.

I am writing because five women a day are murdered by the men who say they love them. I am writing because rape is. I am writing because I am a daughter and a mother and a lover and a sister and a womanist. I am writing to understand. I am writing so I won't be afraid. I am writing so I won't start crying again. I am writing because nobody even said the word sexism to me until I was thirty years old and I want to know why.

I am writing because I have seen my friends bleed to death from illegal abortions. I am writing because I have seen my sisters tortured and tormented by the fathers of their children. I am writing because I almost married a man who beat me regularly and with no remorse. I am writing because my daughter is almost old enough to start "dating" and I don't know how to tell her to protect herself from what I cannot even fully articulate to myself.

I am writing to allow myself to feel the anger. I am writing to keep from running toward it or away from it or into anybody's arms. I am writing to find solutions and pass them on. I am writing to find a language and pass it on.

I am writing, writing, writing, for my life.

Think of this as a workbook.

LAST DAY OF THE YEAR

I s it because we bleed so regularly that everybody thinks we are supposed to?

Is that the reason?

Is it because they can hit us that they do hit us?

She was scrambling around in the back seat. Terrified; clawing at the door; struggling for air in big shuddering gasps; crying; mascara running; hair plastered to her face; her head; her neck; the blond highlights running with the blue shadow.

She was so wet, I thought she was raining.

I thought she was running.

I thought it was a getaway car. Like the one in *Bonnie and Clyde* with people screaming and hollering and second guessing every move they ever made.

We were going to the movies. The three of us. Happy; silly; satisfied. Rounding the corner onto I-20 with no bigger problem than trying to decide where to eat and what to listen to on the radio. Me and Zeke in the front seat, feeling decadent and parental. My daughter in the back seat, fifteen and holding.

I saw him first. Gray pants, beltless and drooping. No shirt. No shoes. Looking for an opening between the cars rushing onto the freeway. I thought he was a young boy, he looked so slender and gangly. Drugs, I thought. This is some drug shit.

I hadn't seen her yet.

I think Zeke saw her first. I know he saw her before I did. I was still looking at the thin brown back of the shirtless man who was running in front of us now, hand out, eyes on fire. Zeke turned the wheel so hard I braced myself for whatever was coming next and then I saw her, off to the left, running. Screaming: "He's got a gun! He's gonna shoot me! Help me! Somebody call the police! He's trying to kill me!"

She was running toward the freeway and away from it at the same time. She was so scared, she didn't care where she was running as long as it was away from the man who was chasing her. But something in her was still frightened enough of the cars whizzing by at seventy miles an hour to hesitate, jerking her back as she tried to will her feet to risk a run into the traffic.

Zeke turned the car again, hard, and I saw the man again, right next to us. Wild-eyed, angry, distracted from the woman by the car aimed at him and gaining. He hit the car with the flat of his hand, jumping back. Zeke put the car in park, unlocked and opened the back door on the side nearest to the woman across from where my daughter sat trying to be invisible and stepped out of the car toward the man the girl was running from.

I saw him do all this as if I was looking through gauze; through rice paper; through the movie screen in silhouette. The woman was screaming.

"Get in the car," I said to her. She just kept screaming. "Get in the car," I said. "Get in the car! Get in the car!"

I could see the man over her shoulder, hurrying away,

looking over his shoulder back toward us. I could feel Zeke more than I could see him. Beside my right shoulder; beyond my left arm; between the man and my daughter. In front of, and behind, and to the side of me. Everywhere and in one place. He was holding a tire iron in his right hand like it was an extension of his arm. Standing between the woman and her running man.

When the man disappeared around a hedge, she finally tumbled into the car, moaning loudly. I locked the door behind her and Zeke got back in beside me and drove smoothly onto the freeway.

The woman was hysterical. Rolling her head around; eyes squeezed tight; moans and small cries and short gasping breaths. She clawed the door like a trapped animal. My daughter's eyes were open wide and she was completely still. I looked at her and she looked back at me.

I reached for the woman's hand tossing and tensing in her lap. "You're okay," I said. "You're okay. You did the right thing. You're okay. You're okay."

I was crooning to her in what my daughter calls "the mother voice." Eminently calm. Unconditionally loving. Understanding of everything. Soothing in a way that has to do with carrying babies inside you. "You're okay," I said again. "You're okay."

She didn't believe me for a second.

"Where are we going?" I said. Zeke was driving. I remember asking because I realized he was not going to the police station, even though she had said, "Call the police!" I remember hoping he wasn't going to double back and look for the guy before I remembered that this was a getaway car.

"Where," I said, "are you driving?"

"No place," he said, very quietly. "I'm just driving."

His voice was completely neutral. He had placed the tire iron back beside the gear shift and he was looking straight ahead. The car moved as if through water. Nothing seemed to make any noise except the woman in the back, weeping and shuddering against the seat. Zeke turned on a tape: The Chambers Brothers, singing about love.

"Open your eyes," I say, still holding her hand. "Look where you are. You're okay. You're okay." I thought she was going to jump out of the car. Still too afraid to sit still for too long. "You're okay," I say again. "You're okay."

She looks at me straight for the first time. "Where do you want us to take you," I say. My timing is off. I made the request too soon. Her eyes panic. "I, I . . ." she is trying to tell me something. "I have asthma," she says, still gasping. "It's okay," I say. "Just relax. Take your time."

She is still holding my hand, but I don't think she knows it. She looks very young. Less than twenty. I could be her mother.

There is a lot of makeup smeared on her face. Tears and snot are everywhere. I hand her a Kleenex and she mops at her face and gulps air, trying to regulate her breathing. She looks at me again and then away.

"Thank you," she says. "Thank you for stopping." She speaks to me, but she means all of us. I nod. Zeke is still driving. She gives me an address not far from where we are. We know exactly where it is. She lives less than three blocks from the house I used to live in with my daughter's father. *In the neighborhood.*

She asks to be let off on the other side of the street and lets my hand go without the sisterly squeeze I want for my own reassurance that she is okay. *Safe.* That someone strong and brave and loving is waiting for her on the other side of that door.

She was really small. High-heeled, thigh-high boots. Skin-tight jeans. Clutching her purse and an old brown sweater. She walked with the mincing little off-balance steps that high-heeled shoes demand and I tried to imagine her running down I-20 in those shoes.

She vomited just outside her apartment door and disappeared inside.

And how can they prey on us and save us, all at the same time?

And how can they possess us and abandon us all at the same time?

And how can we tell the villains from the heroes and the beaters from the leaders and the good guys from the bad guys?

By what they *do*, not what they *say*.

By whether they stop to help, or just drive on.

By whether they are prepared not just to *accept* our anger, but to *share* it and *spare* it and save us from themselves and their brothers gone mad, or *driven* mad, but either way, too mad to figure out how to be with us.

Later, when I kissed my daughter good night, she said, "I am scared to go to sleep. I think something bad is going to happen."

And I kissed her again and assured her in the mother voice that it was the events of the day that were scaring her. That she was safe here in a house with people who loved her and would protect her and could protect her and she didn't need to worry. And she believed me. Because it was true.

So far, so good . . .

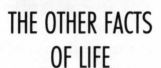

THE OTHER FACTS
OF LIFE

These are the other facts of life. The ones your mother probably didn't tell you because she didn't want to scare you. What she didn't realize was that being scared isn't the most terrible thing that can happen. *Being unprepared is much worse.*

VIOLENCE:

In America, they admit that five women a day are killed by their husbands, boyfriends, ex-husbands, ex-boyfriends or lovers. That doesn't count the women killed during random rapes, murders, robberies and kidnappings.

In America, the main reason women are ever hospitalized is because they've been beaten and tortured by men. More than for childbirth. More than for cancer care. More than from heart attacks.

In America, thousands of women a day are raped and/or tortured and abused by men in as many ways as you can think of, and probably a whole lot more you haven't thought of, and don't want to, including beating, shooting, scalding, stabbing, slapping, shaking and starving.

The facts indicate that we are under siege, incredibly vulnerable, totally unprepared and *too busy denying the truth to collectively figure out what to do about it*. Men beat and torment and rape women because they can. They're usually bigger and physically stronger and they've structured a culture that condones absolutely the possession and control of women by any means necessary.

All this puts us at a tremendous disadvantage, especially since our group is usually fragmented and disorganized. We can't depend on each other for protection yet, and won't be able to until we admit to the problem and then learn something about self-defense. Until that happens, individual knowledge of how to recognize and get out of dangerous situations is crucial to our survival.

All men are *capable* of abusing women, no matter what they tell you or what they call it, so don't kid yourself about this one or that one being different. It takes *years* of love, work, and trust to eliminate the probability of violence in relationships between men and women. *Don't think you can rush the process because you wish you could.*

Don't trust any male strangers. They are guilty until proven innocent. Don't accept rides, favors, gifts, free advice, or compliments from men you don't know. Strangers are always dangerous and friends can be, too, when they are angry, frustrated, confused or crazed by a sexist desire for possession and control of you. (The section on Basic Training has a working definition of the word "sexist" if you don't already have one.)

Learn to recognize these ten early warning signals as a way of anticipating violence in order to avoid it if at all possible:

1. shouting, hollering, excessive cursing, name calling, sarcasm;

2. finger pointing or fist waving, especially in and around your face;

3. arm or wrist grabbing or twisting;

4. throwing or breaking things;

5. hitting his head or his fist against walls, tables, steering wheel, etc., or reckless fast driving;

6. threatening to do violent things to himself, you, your family, your friends, your children;

7. indicating that he has a gun or other weapon;

8. bringing up past arguments or wrongdoing for which he holds you responsible;

9. following you, spying on you, questioning you about your whereabouts or your friends, male or female;

10. locking doors so you are trapped in a car or house and can't leave whenever you want to leave.

If any of these signals occur, stay focused and alert. Do whatever you can to diffuse the situation (short of having a sexual exchange, which is rape) and leave by yourself as soon as possible. Always have cab fare/bus fare/train fare and change for the telephone in your purse. Your life may depend on it.

If this happens in your own house, you should still leave until you can be safe there. Take your children if you can. Go to a friend or a relative. Go to the police station. Go to a fire station (there will always be someone there awake and on duty). Go to a hotel and call for help from the lobby. Tell somebody you need help until you get it.

Violence is never justified. It should never be forgiven. Apologies and pleas for forgiveness should fall on deaf ears. If a man beats you/hits you/shoves you/slaps you/torments you once, *he will do it again.* Cut him loose.

RAPE :

Review the facts at the start of the last section on violence. Let yourself think about them and feel what they really mean to each of us. Keep them in mind while you think about rape.

Rape is a crime of womanhating and violence. It is *not* a crime of passion or a sex crime.

The victim of rape is *never, never, never* responsible, no matter what she was wearing, where she was walking, what she was doing or who she went out with, had a drink with, married, kissed, flirted with or lied to. Bad judgment and carelessness are not punishable by rape.

No rape is ever justified and no rapist has an acceptable reason or excuse. *Ever.*

To protect yourself against being raped by strangers:

1. Secure the place you live with your choice of burglar bars, alarms, dogs, alert neighbors, good lighting and/or a gun you are licensed and trained to use.

2. *Always* lock your car doors and be alert to men on the street when you stop at intersections.

3. Learn to change a tire quickly. Practice doing it in the dark. Don't run out of gas.

4. Try to wait for the bus with a friend or neighbor or coworker especially at night. Avoid waiting or getting off at places where groups of men gather. (Bars, labor pools, shelters, liquor stores, basketball courts, pool halls, etc.)

5. Try not to walk alone at night, but if you have to, walk in the middle of the street so you are in the light and away from the buses and alleys. Keep your hands free and carry Mace.

6. Check for men lurking in underground parking lots, empty buildings and vacant lots.

7. Don't ever accept rides with strangers or men you don't know well enough to trust *absolutely*.

8. Be conscious of the kinds of clothes that men say make them think we want to be raped by them. These include tight pants and sweaters, very high heeled shoes, short skirts, halter tops, see-through clothes, etc.

9. Stay in shape so you can run if you need to run.

10. Practice hollering as loud as you can so you can make a big noise if you are attacked.

To protect yourself from being raped by men you know:

1. Never be alone with a man you don't know well and trust *absolutely*. This takes time. Trust your instincts. Take responsibility for setting the pace and structure of the relationship. Remember the violence warning signals.

2. Don't park or drive in isolated places with men you don't know well and trust absolutely. Whenever possible, take your own car on first dates and drive it yourself.

3. Don't flirt or accept flirting behavior if you're not interested in having sex within the next few hours.

4. Don't go to apartments, houses or hotels with men you don't know well and trust absolutely.

5. Scream and fight back when the first unwelcome sexual approach is made and you realize what is happening. Trust your instincts. *If you think it's happening, it is happening.* Don't wait to protest. Holler. Loud. A "friend" or "date" is less likely to want your noise to draw neighbors, family, friends, police, etc.

6. Don't go out alone with groups of men that you don't know well and trust absolutely. Evaluate each member of the group individually. The men you know well should always outnumber the men you don't know well. Ask *yourself* why

there are no other women there. Ask *them* the same question.

7. Don't watch highly sexual movies, read sexually exciting books or magazines, or talk and tease about sexual things with a man you don't intend to have sex with in the next few hours.

8. Don't kiss and hug and fondle a man you don't intend to have sex with in the next few hours.

9. Don't drink, get high or fall asleep around men you don't know well and trust absolutely.

10. Don't allow any physical contact that you do not initiate, appreciate and fully endorse.

If you are as careful as you can be and you are still attacked and/or raped, *don't panic*. Stay alert. Focus on staying alive and unhurt. Try to remember everything you can about the rapist, the location, the circumstances. As soon as you can, get to safety. Call the police. Call a woman friend to come and be with you. Call your doctor. Call the rape crisis center.

Remember that you are the *victim* and don't take any shit from anybody.

SEX:

Sex is a powerful and basic drive meant to insure the survival of the species. In order to help insure that we Do It, sex can also be pleasurable when it is a voluntary exchange between equals. But sex is not exempt from the madness that is everywhere between men and women. In fact, sex is usually the most volatile and misunderstood battleground of all.

Remember when you think about sex that men often use it to express power, control, womanhating and violence. Phrases like *I knocked the bottom out of it*, and *I fucked her brains out* are the norm, not the exception. Even worse, sex and female sexuality have been tainted, consciously or unconsciously, by male misinterpretation.

Don't be fooled into imitating what you see in the movies, on TV or read in the books that crowd the bestseller lists. Trust yourself. Learn your body. Listen to it. Touch it. Figure out what feels good and what doesn't. Don't confuse pain and pleasure. If it's hurting you, it shouldn't be pleasing him.

Take *complete responsibility* for birth control. Of course, in the best of all possible worlds, men would share equal responsibility for birth control, but, realistically speaking, they won't take it as seriously as we do. They can't get pregnant.

Take *complete responsibility* for safe sex. Protect yourself against AIDS and other sexually transmitted diseases by always carrying and using your own condoms.

Don't fake pleasure, excitement or orgasms. There is no excuse for it, no end to it, and no way to justify it. Whenever you find yourself considering "faking it," ask yourself why and who benefits from such bullshit?

Most of the ways people get together sexually fall into three categories: *mating, making love and having sex.*

Mating is the conscious coupling of two people with the agreed upon intention of having a child. It is the only kind of sexual exchange that can only occur between heterosexuals. "Agreed upon" is the key phrase here. If both people don't agree, the energy won't be in sync and the kid will suffer for it. Also, tricking somebody into bearing or fathering a child when they haven't agreed to it is low down and unfair.

Making Love is communicating sexually on a high physical, mental, emotional and spiritual plane with someone you know, respect, love, trust and desire passionately. Hold out for this kind of sex if you can. Although it is almost impossible to achieve in the midst of the current crisis, it is worth the wait.

Having sex is the catchall description of all the other sexual exchanges that occur and it has several subcategories:

1. *Lustful sex*—this is a purely physical response to another

person. Nothing wrong with it. Be careful about safe sex and birth control. Lust cares nothing for public health questions so plan ahead and come prepared. Lust also gets careless about safety, so review the sections on Rape and Violence.

2. *Sympathy sex*—nothing wrong with this either, except it is often misinterpreted. If the person is so depressed or distraught or disillusioned that sex is the only way you can think of to cheer him/her up (this is *your* idea, right?) then this person is probably in serious need of an anchor, an angel, a savior. What was meant to be simple sympathy sex often ends up with messy misunderstandings on both sides. Avoid it if possible and take your friend out for a cup of cappuccino instead.

3. *Angry sex*—a commonly made mistake, especially in long-term relationships where there isn't enough breathing and pacing room. *Don't do it.* This kind of sex encourages you to use your sexuality in a way that ultimately denies you pleasure and twists your spirit. This kind of sex may also trigger male violence and female depression. *Don't do it.*

4. *Friendship sex*—this can be all right, but it must be controlled by you absolutely. There is a tendency for men who like you to become possessive and controlling once you begin to have friendship sex. Don't act like it's cute when it happens and don't indulge or reward it with more sex. If you value the friendship and you see this happening, stop all sexual activity immediately. Explain why and be unshakable in your decision not to resume sexual relations. Good friends are hard to find.

BASIC TRAINING:
THE BEGINNINGS OF WISDOM

"*W*oman," Japanese feminist/artist Yoko Ono once said, "is the nigger of the world."

I have always found that quote from Yoko offensively interesting. Who was she talking to? The question assumes one cannot be a female and a "nigger" at the same time. Where does that leave black women? Maybe that makes us the *nigger-nigger* of the world. Double niggers. The mind boggles at the kind of oppression that would await such a cursed being. A creature oppressed by racism and sexism, buffeted from niggerhaters to womanhaters and back again with hardly time enough to take a deep breath and try to figure out what to do about it. And to make matters worse, the poor doomed thing lives in America. I would suspect even Yoko Ono's fertile imagination could not conceive of such a fate.

I know the feeling. Last summer, I opened the morning newspaper to read that a twelve-year-old black girl had been discovered last evening by her mother, lying dead in the middle of the living room floor, her face beaten to a bloody pulp, her jump rope tied around her neck and a broom handle rammed up into her vagina. The crime took place during

daylight hours in a heavily trafficked area of a crowded apartment complex, but nobody saw anything or anybody
unusual. As I write these words, almost a year later, the
murderer is still at large.

When I read that story, the first thing I felt was fear. Had
things gotten so bad that the fiend who was capable of com-
mitting such a crime could blend into our neighborhoods
without causing a ripple? The thought was chilling, especially
since the summer had been filled with news reports of an
escalating wave of black male violence directed primarily
toward black women and children on the streets, in their
cars, in their own homes.

A series of murders of elderly black women raped and
strangled in their beds. A black mother kidnapped at the bus
stop and sodomized on the nearby railroad tracks in full view
of her screaming baby daughter. Black women snatched off
the street by a rapist who gouged out their right eyes to
subdue them. Ex-wives and estranged lovers stalked and shot
down outside their jobs by the men they used to sleep with.
And now this last one, too horrible to be ignored or explained
away, no matter how they tried to sanitize it for the six
o'clock news.

I had never felt quite so frightened; quite so helpless; quite
so *angry*. But angry at who and for what and in what context?
As if on cue, the chorus of smoothly cautionary black male
voices that live inside my head spoke as one.

Surely I couldn't condemn *all* black men for the murder-
ous violence of a few "bad apples." Surely I wouldn't be so
hysterical as to label *all* black men dangerous because there
were some criminals among their number. Surely I understood the danger and divisiveness of perpetrating such "negative images" of black men. Surely I wasn't so ignorant of our
history as to decry the horror of these crimes without placing
the ultimate blame where it belonged, on white racism and

the unfocused, but *understandable*, anger it produces in black men. Surely I am clear that it is not "the brothers" who are the problem. It's "the Man." Right?

Wrong. It's the brothers. Period. Although all African American insanity, male and female, can ultimately be explained by the long ago presence of the slave ships pulling up on the coast of Africa, that blood soaked presence cannot continue to be an acceptable reason for our current sorry state. We cannot undo slavery. It happened. We cannot ignore racism. It is a fact of our lives. But we can begin to work on the ways that racism makes us turn on each other. Black men must begin to take *personal responsibility* for the way they treat us and the way they treat our children.

There is no white man physically present in the house when a black man decides to beat his wife. There is no white man present when black men prey on women old enough to be their grandmothers to get money for crack. There is no white man present when black girls are not safe from rape in their own neighborhoods or in their own front rooms. There is no white man present at the conception of a black baby, who will be born with AIDS because the father has been sharing needles.

And, *yes*, I really do understand that white men are responsible for the madness, but who is responsible for the cure?

I also understand that racism is a heavy burden to bear and can make black men feel mean and hostile and crazy because it makes black women feel crazy, too.

And I understand that white men are hard to work for, hard to live around, hard to pass on the street and hard to figure out a way around because all that is hard for black women, too.

And I understand the danger of being black in America where white men control the guns because that is dangerous for black women, too.

I understand the frustration of last hired, first fired because black women are the only group in the nation with worse employment statistics than black men in *every* category and at *every* wage level. (Bitter, unprovable-by-any-statistics-anywhere accusations by brothers who tell us that being black and female gives us an unfair advantage in the marketplace notwithstanding.)

I understand the horror of poor health care and its attendant ills because black women have the worst health profile of any group in the United States.

I understand it's hard trying to make ends meet, get ahead in the world, be a good person, find time for yourself, love your children, and be active in your community because we have a hard time with all that, too.

I understand and experience all the dangers and frustrations and limitations of being black in America because I am black in America. Black *and* female. Being black and male isn't any worse. It's just *different.* Brothers who try to make a case for black men suffering more keenly from the effects of racism than black women are either lying or misinformed.

Besides, it is a no-win competition. They get shot more; we get raped regularly. They do more heroin; we're into crack. We're *all* in terrible shape because of the presence of racism and sexism in our lives. Debate about who is the most victimized victim doesn't take us anywhere but deeper into victimhood and is usually a smoke screen thrown up by brothers in an effort to keep the discussion focused on *race* and not on *gender.*

Sexism is still not a word that gets used much in the black community, even though it describes a form of oppression that effects the majority population of the community—women!—and is no less virulent and deadly than racism. This other "ism" is real, present and provable, just like racism. It oppresses black women with depressing and dependable regularity, just like racism, and it has been thoroughly documented as a fact of American life. Just like racism.

In spite of this overload of available information, most black men won't even admit to the existence of sexism, certainly not within their own communities and almost never in their own lives. They won't entertain serious discussion of it or accept it as a fact of life within every black household in the country.

The fact that black men routinely and cavalierly deny something that is a critical element in our African American female reality makes us feel crazy since it seems so clear to us we don't understand why *they* can't see it. It also robs us of the possibility of working cooperatively with our brothers on defining the problem and trying to solve it. If black men won't admit that their sexism and male chauvinism and domestic violence are problems, how can we consider them allies in the search for creative solutions?

We can't. Not yet. Not until they are willing to redefine their black male reality to incorporate the equally valid reality of our black female experiences. Not until they are prepared to recognize and admit to their role as oppressors in the struggle against sexism and see their crimes as no less serious than the crimes committed in defense of racism.

This is a difficult process, made no less difficult by the fact that we, black women, have no adequate language with which to *describe* our situation, to ourselves or to anyone else. Most of us have accepted black men's indifference to or hostility toward sexism as good enough reasons to ignore the problem. We therefore don't even have working definitions of the words needed to begin to articulate our specific black female reality.

Our history of thinking about struggle is so shaped by our experiences with white American racism that when we begin to talk about oppression we invariably get sidetracked into talking about racism *only*. We are, of course, encouraged in this by The Brothers, who much prefer the more familiar and acceptable status of oppressed victim to the less admirable role of the violent oppressor.

As a result of this absence of regular, widely accessible discussion on the subject of sexism and how it messes up our lives, many intelligent, aware, politically conscious black men and women go through their lives with no working definitions of the basic concepts which establish the context for any serious struggle against sexism; no continuing dialogue with each other about that struggle; and no mutually accepted standard against which to evaluate their own behavior and the behavior of others. In the swirl of our collective ignorance, no clarity is possible, no dialogue productive, and the problem goes undefined.

An old Chinese proverb says that the beginning of wisdom is to call all things by their proper names. The process of naming and defining begins the process of discovery. It is in that spirit that I offer Basic Training.

Basic Training is useful for personal discovery or review, helpful in discussions with your sisters and *critical* to the creative enlightenment of The Brothers. No black woman should attempt to discuss anything about sexism with a black man before he has mastered the basics. Such a discussion is doomed to failure and holds the potential for sparking anger and non-productive exchanges.

Moreover, any black man who will not take the time to master Basic Training isn't being serious about a question we've already said is life and death to us and he doesn't deserve your time, your attention and your lovingkindness.

The following ten basic definitions, concepts and approaches together make up Basic Training. Here they are:

1. *Sexism*—all the ways men mess over women from the cradle to the grave and which are painfully evident in all

rituals, institutions, educational systems, cultural expressions, family structures, religions and economic systems that men have devised; a social relationship in which males have authority over females.

It is *impossible* to live in America and not be tainted by sexism *and* a participant in it, either as a victim or a perpetrator. As women, by the end of our African American girlhoods, we have learned and perfected a dizzying variety of slave behaviors which we are rewarded for mastering by the men who made them up in the first place.

As men, they were taught that we were inferior, unworthy of their respect, subject to their whim and present on earth primarily for their sexual pleasure and the bearing and mothering of their children.

We were *all* taught that it is acceptable for them to hit us when they think we have "asked for it" and that their opinions carry more weight in all critical decisions simply because they are men and therefore assumed to be of superior knowledge and more vast experience.

2. *Sexist*—a person who practices *sexism*, consciously or unconsciously, by living in a way that endorses, perpetuates and prolongs it. *All* men—including black men—born and raised in America are sexists, even those who are consciously struggling against it. Men are never completely cured of sexism. They can, however, consciously and consistently alter their behavior. Sort of like recovering alcoholics.

An integral part of that recovery process is the admission of culpability, responsibility and the element of choice. Ignorance of the problem, feigned or real, is no excuse for inaction. Men run the world. The fact that they are oppressing women can't have just slipped by them. The means to stop the problem are within their control. If they don't do it, it's because they don't *want* to do it.

Black men, because they are oppressed and influenced by

white men, often express their sexism in ways identical to the ways the white men they so despise express racism. The irony of this is usually lost on black men but should make it clear to us that there is a big difference between clarity on *race* and clarity on sexism. The two are definitely related and usually complementary, but absolutely *not* interchangeable.

3. *Feminism*—the belief that women are full human beings capable of participation and leadership in the full range of human activities—intellectual, political, social, sexual, spiritual and economic. Feminism is to sexism what black nationalism is to racism; the most rational response to the problem.

4. *Feminist*—a woman who believes in and practices *feminism* in working to eliminate her own internalized sexism and the sexism of those around her. Although men are allowed to call themselves "feminists" in some of the more liberal circles, I do not endorse this practice. Men can be enlightened, but I have never met a man who did not cling to and exemplify sexist behavior from time to time in spite of himself. Letting them dub themselves "feminists" tends to lead to smugness, self-satisfaction and the feeling that the man who is struggling to overcome his own sexism and the sexism of his brothers has somehow achieved a more exalted status, a safe conduct pass that allows him to be a little less rigorous on himself, having demonstrated his good intentions. I am reminded of my grandmother's admonition about what paves the road to hell.

5. *Racist* is to black people what *sexist* is to women; The Enemy. Race plays a major role in our perceptions about sexism, our strategies for fighting against it, and black men's primarily unenlightened responses to examinations of the question, especially those that include discussion of their own sexist behavior. Racism adds a layer of anger and stress in our lives as black people that makes it even more difficult for us to take on the responsibility of fighting yet another

deadly "ism." Struggling against sexism as part of a group that is also racially oppressed is like walking to work with bad feet: you know you have to do it, but those bunions make the journey just that much harder.

But in trying to talk to black men about sexism (or to understand it more clearly ourselves) our racial history is an invaluable tool. Black men who have experienced racism are already familiar with what oppression *looks* like, how it *operates*, how it can permeate and poison every area of your life. The problem is, we have not figured out a way to use that racial knowledge to help them understand sexism and their role in it.

Let me explain: By the time I was eight or nine, I understood clearly that slavery and racism had created a complex set of circumstances that impacted daily on my life as an African American. Factors such as where I lived, how I lived, what jobs I could get, how clean the grocery stores were in my neighborhood, the probability that I'd get robbed and raped were all in some way circumscribed by the presence of white racism.

I also knew that as a person who had the advantage of growing up in a house where there were books, it was my responsibility once I achieved adulthood to work consciously to "uplift the race," or at least as much of it as I could, given limited resources, human frailty, and the awesome implacability of the group itself.

I also had a world view through which to filter the complex racial stimuli that I was receiving from books, from teachers and from the media. I knew that every aberrant form of African American behavior could be understood—not *justified* but completely understood—by admitting to the reality of the slave ship; to the raping of wives in front of their husbands; to the selling of babies torn from their mothers' arms. My family made it clear to me that there was no way we as a people could recover from such barbarism and injustice in less than 200 years. Complete clarity on that basic point was necessary to establish a context for understanding why black folks do the things we do and being able to love us anyway.

I also had another invaluable tool for understanding my position as an oppressed African American—*a definable adversary*. White racism, represented and perpetrated by white people through a maze of institutions, laws and customs they are prepared to defend with their lives and, whenever possible, *our* lives. I understood that white people had been raised by their culture to be racist in order to maintain status and control and I was encouraged to question everything they did or said since it was never going to be in my best interest to believe them without checking some reliable black source first, preferably my family since they had a vested interest in my not acting a fool.

All this critical information and racial analysis was presented to me as an integral part of my daily life, not a special ceremony during Black History Month. These African American survival lessons were part of the fabric of family; expected, accepted and continuous.

A good example of this routine is the running commentary my politically radical and highly opinionated family would offer during the nightly news. I grew up, in fact, hearing two news casts. The one the white male TV newscaster (they were all white males back then) was giving and the one my family was giving in a kind of sepia-toned simulcast.

When the newsguy said something critical about Patrice Lumumba, my mother reminded him that the Belgians used to cut off the hands of captured Africans in order to terrorize them into being slaves. When the guy said something sketchy about the reasons for a recent violent crime wave in the black community, my stepfather filled in the missing pieces and then wondered aloud who had put this fool on the air anyway.

In this way, I learned early to have no respect for what white men said about being black, and, by extension, about anything else. This self-confidence and clarity grew directly out of my racial self-awareness and gave me a powerful tool for understanding the seemingly random and increasingly frightening events of the sixties. I had an oppressed person's most potent weapons: information, analysis and positive group identity.

As I began to seriously understand what it meant to be black *and* female in America, the tools my family gave me for the development of a black consciousness were, and are, invaluable. But how do we transfer racial understanding to a discussion of sexism? What is the process by which we can use what we know about being *black* to understand and articulate what we know about being black *women*?

The next three basics should help us begin that delicate process.

6. *Racism* and *sexism* are systems of oppression designed to control, confine and exploit one group of people (the *oppressed*) for the benefit of another group of people (the *oppressor*). In discussions of *sexism*, black women are the oppressed and black men are the oppressors.

7. *Sexism* operates a lot like *racism* except it is based on sexual identity instead of racial identity. Women of *all* social and economic classes are oppressed by sexism.

8. In discussions of *race* between black people and white people, the conscious black person is *always* right; is *always* the ultimate authority on questions having to do with race and racism; must *always* be regarded as the "injured party," or the oppressed. The reason for this is obvious. It is in the best interest of white people to keep black people oppressed. They cannot possibly be expected to be objective about ques-

tions of race and should therefore adopt a *listening*, not a speaking posture. *Nic*

9. In discussions of *sexism*, the conscious woman is *always* right; *always* the ultimate authority on questions having to do with sexism; *always* the "injured party," or oppressed. The reasons for this are obvious. It is in men's best interest to keep women oppressed and under their control. They cannot be expected to be objective—no matter how loudly and self-righteously they protest—about questions of sexism and should therefore adopt a *listening* rather than a speaking posture.

This last Basic may be the most difficult of all for black men to deal with. The idea of agreeing in *advance* that a black woman will be the ultimate and final authority on all questions regarding any subject is inconceivable to most black men. They are convinced they know more than we do about everything—*even about us!*—and most black men will argue and pout and rant and rave about how stupid, unfair, unacceptable and unenlightened such a condition is. Let him vent for an appropriate but not self-indulgent amount of time and then ask him how many times he has let a white man tell him *anything* about what it feels like to be a black man. If he hesitates, refer him back to Basic number 7.

See what I mean about how helpful the racial comparison can be?

One cautionary note: Honest discussions of sexism are always emotionally intense no matter what the sex of the participants. Exchanges between men and women on sexism and related topics are especially charged. Understanding this reality, it is important to establish that in addition to always being *right*, the black women involved in such discussions have the right to establish the acceptable vocabulary and appropriate level of emotional and physical response in *any and all* discussions with The Brothers about matters regarding any aspect of sexism.

So, last but not least, Basic number 10:

10. No hollering, waving of arms or objects in a threatening or excited manner, cursing and name calling during discussions of sexism and sexist behavior without explicit permission from the Sister in control, as in this exchange:

Brother: "May I throw this tape player across the room in your direction to show my anger at your defining me as a sexist and perhaps intimidate you into being quiet by introducing the possibility of violence into this exchange?"

Sister says: "No, and please stop pounding your fist against the wall while we talk."

The reason, again, is obvious. Domestic violence is the front line of the war against women. Black men, consciously and unconsciously, use the threat of violence, the fact of their superior strength and their well-known volatility to keep black women nervous and frightened. A man who will holler and throw things at you or around you when there is a disagreement has already introduced violence into the environment. He will probably also feel that he can grab you, push you, or shake his fingers or fist in your face. *This is dangerous, oppressive, sexist behavior.* Ask him to stop, explaining why if you can. If he doesn't stop, or becomes more threatening or exasperated or coldly sarcastic, end the discussion as neutrally as possible and then find some quiet time alone to evaluate the brother's actions and your appropriate response.

It is important to remember that men beat and kill women *regularly*. The threat and the *actuality* of violence are the keys to male domination and control of women. Most black men, having been raised in a sexist country, have at some level absorbed the acceptability of violence against women. Be alert. Take responsibility for monitoring the emotional level of the discussions and controlling it. It is our *safety* and well being that are at stake.

If your efforts at discussing these questions honestly continue to degenerate into emotionally or potentially physically violent episodes, ask yourself why you continue to try to have the discussion with someone who isn't interested. Give yourself an honest answer and then decide how to proceed.

One final note: During the discussions that will accompany mastering the Basics, some brothers may attempt to speak to you in what I have named "mantones." This is the tone of voice regularly used by men to address women and children and other perceived inferiors. (For example, *white* men use *mantones* to speak to *black* men, but *black* men don't get to use *mantones* when speaking to *white* men.)

Other distinguishing features are the assumption of all available authority and an unshakeable belief in the superiority of male moral fiber. A mantone is always condescending, often sarcastic and has been known to reduce grown women to weeping and cursing wrecks with its implacable certainty and smug inability to *listen* to anything a woman has to say.

Mantones are by their very nature and intent oppressive, sexist, *learned* behavior. They can be unlearned once they are defined and mutually accepted as unacceptable behavior.

Most women are aware of mantones although we have not had a word to describe them clearly, making it impossible to get any agreement on outlawing them. The Brothers may have a difficult time understanding the concept of mantones, but once you have had some initial discussion, you can begin to point the tones out to him whenever they occur—in him, in the media, in his friends, etc. Simply reference your initial discussion and point out the example. As in: "Remember the other day when we were talking about mantones? Well, this is one."

Examples will be *everywhere* and as he begins to understand the whole idea and hear the arrogance and obnoxious-ness of mantones for himself, a brother of good heart will begin to work seriously to eliminate his own mantones as quickly as possible.

It will be helpful to review Basic number nine before be-ginning the discussion of mantones to eliminate unnecessary objections to the obvious.

MAD AT MILES

I thought I wasn't going to be able to write this piece at all.
I had been avoiding it for a month. Trying to think of
something else to say. Something funny. After all, we are
gathered here to celebrate our creative genius. Not to talk
about men beating women and five-a-day domestic murders
and all that "sexist shit."

That wasn't the reason I almost didn't do the piece,
though. I almost didn't do the piece because I thought Miles
Davis had put a hex on me. I thought somehow he had found
out that I was writing a piece suggesting that *he is guilty of
self-confessed violent crimes against women such that we should
break his albums, burn his tapes and scratch up his CDs until he
acknowledges and apologizes and rethinks his position on The
Woman Question.*

That sounds terrible doesn't it? Breaking Miles Davis records? Because of a few mistakes in his personal life? Next
thing you know, I'll be fussing about 2 Live Crew just because they don't know the difference between rape and reciprocity . . .

But I'm getting ahead of myself. I hadn't even written the

piece yet. I was just thinking about it. Well, I was a little closer than that. I was sitting down to write it, but I needed to have the records. The albums in my own collection that would provide my personal connection to the subject. I needed to hear the music playing beside me in order to remember why I had been avoiding this question so energetically. And why I was so mad at Miles.

I remembered distinctly, one evening, several months ago when I was feeling particularly well organized, I pulled out the five Miles Davis records that I own and put them aside until it was time to write. But when I needed them back, I couldn't find them anywhere. I looked in all the places where they should have been. Nothing.

Finally on my third trip down to the basement for one last look, a thought popped into my mind that made my blood run cold. He knows! Miles Davis made my records disappear because somebody told him I was going to write a piece that said *he is guilty of self-confessed violent crimes against women such that we should break his albums, burn his tapes and scratch up his CDs until he acknowledges and apologizes and agrees to rethink his position on The Woman Question.*

Didn't sound quite as bad that time, did it? The idea of it, I mean. Just the idea that we could hold a black man responsible for crimes against black women. It's still a pretty heady thought, though, and not necessarily one I thought Miles would endorse, especially since he is the one I'm so mad at.

But there's a reason for that! He's the one who admitted to it. Almost bragged about it. He's the one who confessed in print and then proudly signed his name. Nobody was ever able to show me where David Ruffin admitted to hitting Tammi Terrell in the head with a hammer, even though on the West Side of Detroit where I grew up we had all heard it from somebody who said it like they had the inside line on such things.

And nobody was able to provide me with a quote from Bill Withers describing how he beat up Denise Nicholas when their marriage was grinding to a painfully public close although people tell me *Jet* covered the whole episode in great and gory detail.

But Miles . . . well, I'll let the brother speak for himself. This is an excerpt from *Miles: The Autobiography* by Miles Davis with Quincy Troupe:

Cicely was especially jealous of a woman taking her place in my life, but after a while she didn't have no place in my life, even though she turned down a lot of movie offers just to stay around me. Cicely's like two different women, one nice, the other one totally fucked up. For example, she used to bring her friends around anytime she wanted, but she didn't want my friends coming around. And she had some friends who I couldn't stand. One time we argued about one friend in particular, and I just slapped the shit out of her. She called the cops and went down into the basement and was hiding there. When the police came, they asked me where she was. I said, "She's around here someplace. Look down in the basement." The cop looked in the basement and came back and said, "Miles, nobody's down there but a woman, and she won't talk to me. She won't say nothing."

So I said, "That's her, and she's doing the greatest acting job ever." Then the cop said he understood—she didn't look like she was hurt or nothing. I said, "Well, she ain't hurt bad; I just slapped her once."

The cop said, "Well, Miles, you know when we get these calls we have to investigate."

"Well, if she's beating my ass you gonna come with your guns ready, too?" I asked him.

"They just laughed and left. Then I went down and told Cicely, "I told you to tell your friend not to call over here no more. Now if you don't tell him, I'm gonna tell him." She ran to the phone and called him up and told him, "Miles don't want me talking to you anymore." Before I knew it, I had slapped her again. So she never did pull that kind of shit on me again.

The truth is, this is all my friend A.B.'s fault. It was wintertime. My train got into D.C. early and I caught the Metro out to his house. By the time I got there, there was a fire in the fireplace, his wife Karen was up drinking coffee and the kids were wandering around in their nightgowns, demanding breakfast.

Karen and A.B.'s house used to be a nun's dormitory and they still have a built-in receptacle for Holy Water in the room where A.B. keeps his records, which is only fitting since A.B. has the most *divine* records of anybody I have ever known. Most of them are so rare and hard to find that you can't even think about stealing them because when he spots them at your house later, you'd have to say something lame and unconvincing like: "Yeah, man, I was really lucky to find that record of the Brazilian drummers. I know! Just like that one you used to have before you lost it." You wouldn't have a chance.

And A.B. doesn't just have a lot of records, he knows a lot about music, most especially about jazz. Which is why I asked him to suggest something that might help me understand about trumpets. I didn't make it any more specific than that because it wasn't any more specific than that. I wanted to understand as much about trumpets as I had learned about saxophones from talking to A.B. about John Coltrane.

I was an innocent. He could have given me anybody. But he gave me Miles Davis. *Kind of Blue*. And he didn't even warn me that *Miles was guilty of self-confessed violent crimes against women such that we ought to break his records, burn his tapes and scratch up his CDs until he acknowledges and apologizes and agrees to rethink his position on The Woman Question.*

(It gets easier to say the more you say it. It's starting to sound almost legitimate, isn't it?)

I know I was late, the album having been recorded in March of 1959 when I was only eleven years old and if Smokey Robinson wasn't singing it, there was no way I was going to hear it, and this being the late seventies and all, but I didn't care. I was amazed by the music. I loved it, listened to it, couldn't get enough. A.B. was pleased that his choice had been the right one and he taped the record for me before I left so I could listen to it on the train.

Which is, of course, what I did. I spent the night curled up in my tiny roomette watching America roll by outside my window and listening to Miles Davis play me into the next phase of my life.

The Bohemian Woman Phase. The single again after a decade of married phase. The last time I had a date I was eighteen and oh, god, now I'm thirty phase. The in need of a current vision of who and what and why I am phase. The cool me out quick cause I'm hanging by a thread phase.

For this frantic phase, Miles was perfect. Restrained, but hip. Passionate, but cool. He became a permanent part of the seduction ritual. Chill the wine. Light the candles. Put on a little early Miles. Give the gentleman caller an immediate understanding of what kind of woman he was dealing with. This was not a woman whose listening was confined to the vagaries of the Top 40. This was a woman with the *possibility* of an interesting past, and the *probability* of an interesting future.

This was the woman I was learning to be, and I will confess that I spent many memorable evenings sending messages of great personal passion through the intricate improvisations of *Kind of Blue* when blue was the furthest thing from my mind and Miles, like I said, was perfect.

But I didn't know then that *he was guilty of self-confessed violent crimes against women such that we ought to break his records, burn his tapes and scratch up his CDs until he acknowledges and apologizes and agrees to rethink his position on The Woman Question.*

Still sounds pretty scary, doesn't it? Scratching up CDs and burning cassettes. Pretty right-wing stuff, I know, but what are we going to do? Either we think it's a crime to hit us or we don't. Either we think our brothers have to take responsibility for stopping the war against us, or we don't.

And if we do, can we keep giving our money to Miles Davis so that he can buy a Malibu beach house and terrorize our sisters in it?

Can we make love to the rhythms of "a little early Miles" when he may have spent the morning of the day he recorded the music slapping one of our sisters in the mouth?

Can we continue to celebrate the genius in the face of the monster?

When I asked a musician friend of mine if he had read the letter in a national magazine from a woman who said Miles had settled out of court with her in a suit charging him with extreme physical and mental cruelty during the course of their lengthy professional friendship and subsequent love affair, my friend the musician said, *"Is that the one he beat up at the airport?"*

As opposed, I guess, to the one he beat up in her apartment, or in the backseat of his limo. Or, well, you can see how complicated the problem gets . . .

I tried to just forget about it. But that didn't work. I kept thinking about Cicely Tyson hiding in the basement of her house while the police were upstairs laughing with Miles. I wondered what she was thinking about, crouched down there in the darkness. I wondered if thinking about his genius made her less frightened and humiliated.

I wondered if his genius made it possible for her to forgive him for *self-confessed violent crimes against women such that we ought to break his records, burn his tapes and scratch up his CDs until he acknowledges and apologizes and agrees to rethink his position on The Woman Question.*

(Didn't sound bad at all that time, did it?)

I wondered if she tried to remember the last time she had known a brother whose genius was not in the way he played a horn, or made a living or ran a city, but in the way he loved her.

The danger is that we have gone so long without asking the question that we have forgotten the answer.

The danger is that we have gone so long taking what we can get that we have forgotten what we wanted.

But I can't stop thinking about it. I can't stop wondering what we would do if the violence was against black men instead of black women. Would we forgive the perpetrator so quickly and allow him into our private time; our spiritual moments; our sweet surrenders?

I can't stop wondering what our reaction would be if, say, Kenny G—a resourceful, crossover white male who is selling well enough in our community these days to tie with Anita Baker and Luther Vandross as the seduction music of choice for black urban professionals between the ages of twenty and forty-five . . .

. . . What if Kenny G was revealed to be kicking black men's asses all over the country in between concert appearances and recording sessions?

What if Kenny G wrote a book saying that sometimes he had to slap black men around a little just to make them cool out and leave him the fuck alone so he could get some peace and quiet?

What if Kenny G said this black man who saved his life and rescued his work and restored his mind pissed him off so bad one day he had to slap the shit out of him? *Twice.*

Would Kenny G be the music we would play to center and calm ourselves?

Would Kenny G be the music we would play to relax and focus the person we love on romance?

Would Kenny G be the music we would play when our black male friends came to call?

And if we did and they questioned us about it—and you know they would question us about it!—would we explain our continuing support of Kenny G's music by saying: "Yeah, I know he's beating black men and all that, but this white boy is a musical genius! I don't let personal stuff get in the way of my appreciation of his music. After all, the brothers probably asked for it. You know how it is when y'all start naggin' and shit."

So the question is: How can they hit us and still be our heroes?

And the question is: How can they hit us and still be our leaders? Our husbands?

Our lovers? Our geniuses? Our friends?

And the answer is . . . they can't.

Can they?

GOOD BROTHER BLUES

I spend a lot of time talking to my sisters, and in between raising our children and earning our livings and struggling for our freedom and loving our womenfriends and building a new world, we *sometimes*—every now and then—talk about the brothers.

Invariably the discussion moves from vivid descriptions of the various ways in which the brothers stray far and wide from our definition of what constitutes "a good brother," to wistful expressions of disbelief at the unrelenting shortage in this area, to a resigned sigh and the unspoken question of why there seem to be so many more good sisters than there are good brothers.

Now I will admit that these are complex questions to consider, but how can we arrive at the correct position on the issues of the day without confronting them? Is Marion Barry, for example, "a good brother" with a few personal problems, under siege from the forces of racism and evil, or a physically abusive womanhater who regularly lied to his wife, manipulated his female employees and acquaintances, and backhanded his lover so hard he knocked her down before she had ever even met any FBI agents?

See what I mean about the complexity of the questions? But I am optimistic. I believe we can work it out. I believe we have to and that time is getting very short . . .

So, as part of that move toward clarity, I offer the following Report from the Front Lines as part of our continuing examination of whatever it is that is going on between black men and black women.

Our latest research indicates that part of the problem is that most brothers don't have any clear idea of what we think a good brother is. This means that there is a strong possibility that it is their confusion, not their ill will, that makes the gulf so wide between us and them.

Perhaps the problem is that we haven't given them a current, updated, cross-referenced definition to work with. Maybe they are just sort of marking time, following their own black male instincts, until we reach consensus and begin to spread the good word.

And maybe, in this terrible vacuum of values and standards, they are simply following the lead of their white male counterparts, a thuggish group of violent, homophobic, womanhating, ne'er-do-wells, whose commitment to sexism is matched only by their absolute dedication to racism and their continuing quest to control as much of the world as they can get their greedy, warmongering hands on.

Assuming this is the case—and I know this comes under the category of giving the brothers the benefit of the doubt, but we have almost nothing left to lose and everything to gain —so *assuming* this is the case, I think it is time we put forward a working definition of who and what we are looking for.

We are looking for a good brother.

We are looking for a righteous brother. A *real* righteous

brother. Not one of those singing white guys who made the loss of love sound so intensely intense that you had to fall in love every time the record came on.

We are looking for a real righteous brother. An all grown up, ain't scared of nuthin', and knows it's time to save the race righteous brother.

A good father/good husband/good lover/good worker/good warrior/serious revolutionary righteous brother.

A tuck the baby in at night and accept equal responsibility for child raising and household maintenance chores righteous brother.

A generate a regular paycheck *or* provide evidence of mutually agreed upon, full-time alternative service to the race or to the family, such as playing a saxophone or writing novels, or providing community defense, or taking primary responsibility for children's nurturing and education righteous brother.

A read a book and play a tune and dance your slow dance sweet and low down righteous brother.

A love black women, protect black children and never hit a woman righteous brother.

A turn the TV off and let's talk instead righteous brother.

A turn the TV off and let's make love instead righteous brother.

A stay at home 'cause that's where you wanna be righteous brother.

A brother who can listen.

A brother who can teach.

A brother who can change. For the better.

A brother who can move. Toward the center of the earth.

A brother who is not intimidated or confused by the power and the magic of women.

We are looking for a righteous brother. What we used to call *a good brother.*

A brother who loves his people.

A brother who doesn't hit or holler at or shoot or stab or grab or shove or kick or shake or slap or punch women or children.

A brother who doesn't call women hoes, bitches, skanks, pussies, dykes, sluts, cunts, etc., etc., etc.

A brother who knows there is no such thing as a rape joke.

A brother who uses condoms without being asked.

A brother who doesn't call sex screwing.

A brother who knows that time and tenderness are more important than size and speed and that reciprocity is everything.

A brother who knows that permission must be gained at every step before proceeding.

A brother who doesn't describe the details of an intimate heterosexual encounter by saying, "Man, I knocked the bottom out of it." Or: "I fucked her brains out." Or: "I drew blood from that bitch."

A brother who says: "I made her feel good. I showed her how much I love and cherish her."

A brother who says: "I rubbed warm oil on her."

A brother who says: "I kissed every part of her I could kiss."

A brother who says: "I made her feel so safe and happy and free that she fell asleep in my arms and her heart beat sounded like the ocean after a storm . . ."

We are looking for a real good brother.

We are looking for a brother who will turn the ships around.

Now I know the whole boat question is a Serious Manhood Thing, and I know how dangerous it can be to offer an opinion about any topic that falls within their sacred circle, but I'll risk it for the sake of clarification. We can't afford to have any further confusion on these questions of what does and does not constitute manhood. Not from our side any-way.

In doing the necessary research to put forward our working definition of a good brother, it came to my attention that some brothers feel that we, their sisters, are giving mixed signals when it comes to the manhood thing. We want, they say, all the protection and safety offered by a strong man, but we are unwilling to accept the presence of the warrior's heart.

We, they say, are responsible for any confusion that exists on the manhood question; we are the ones, they say, that counsel caution instead of courage; diplomacy instead of defense.

They say that when the ships pulled up on the shores of Africa and the slavers came ashore to look for us, we were the ones who held them back; the ones who told them that it might be dangerous to go down to the water's edge.

We were the ones, they say, who encouraged them to stay at home, telling them how worried we would be if they went down there with the other warriors to turn the ships around, assuring them that if they just sat here by the fire with us, the white folks would probably change their minds and go away all by themselves. They say that's the reason why they didn't turn the ships around. Because they thought we didn't want them to.

Assuming this is a correct presentation of herstorical fact (and I am unconvinced), it is clearly one of the greatest examples of miscommunication in all of human herstory and one we should avoid repeating at all costs.

So let it be known that we are looking for a brother who will turn the ships around.

A brother who will go into the crack house and turn the ships around.

A brother who will go to the places where it is open season on our children and turn the ships around.

A brother who will hear the screams of sisters beaten to death by the men who say they love them and turn the ships around.

A brother who will hear the whimper of our babies born with AIDS and turn the ships around.

A brother who will see the people sleeping on the street and turn the ships around.

A brother who will remember how freedom feels and turn the ships around.

A brother who will gather with the warriors and march down to the edge of the sea and turn the ships around/turn the ships around/turn the ships around/and this time, turn the ships around . . .

PART TWO

FATAL FLOOZIES

OUT HERE ON OUR OWN

I t is a dangerous time to be a black woman in America. It's a time when we are not safe in the streets or at home or at school or at work and nobody seems to be able to do anything about it. Nobody. Not us. Not our mommas. Not the police. Not the people we elected to look out for our interests. Nobody. We're just out here.

We're just out here, watching our children get shot in their sleep or raped in their living rooms or stomped in the hallways of their high schools. We're out here, helpless and unprotected, while a generation of angry, dispossesed black men, for whom the future holds no possibilities of even minimum wage jobs, turn on us with breathtaking viciousness and no sense of anything besides the necessity to "get paid."

We're just out here, reflecting more and more the madness all around us; abandoning our crack-addicted babies in the crowded hallways of charity hospitals or selling our preteen daughters to the crackman in exchange for a few more rocks; catching AIDS at a faster rate than any other segment of the population from men who forget to tell us they are bisexual or dope fiends or just careless.

We're just out here, being tortured and tormented and murdered by the men who said they loved us and fathered our children and married us or moved in with us and then decided somewhere along the way that they would break our jaws or crack our ribs or knock our teeth out for whatever reason seemed to them acceptable at the time. And when we call for help, the police don't want to come because everybody knows how dangerous that kind of call can be, and even if they do come and take him away, he probably won't be in jail long enough to do anything but get even madder so he can come back here and kick in the door and we can start all over again.

We're just out here making that daily mad dash from the bus stop to our apartment doors, panting and breathing over our shoulders as we fumble the key into the lock, wishing the city would repair the streetlight one day and hoping the rapist or the junkie or the murderer isn't already inside, hiding and waiting for us to lock ourselves in before we realize our mistake.

We're just out here, weeping in full-color photographs on the front page of the daily newspaper, tearing our hair out on the six o'clock news, trying to hold it together at the funerals that are now our most regular gathering place, and begging for meetings with elected officials who only address us after the election is over in the roundabout way of those who wish we'd stop being such a problem all the time and *get with the program*. You don't want the six o'clock news showing everybody a whole bunch of disagreeable black women, do you?

Yes. I do. I want *everyone* to see a bunch of *extremely* disagreeable, screaming, hollering, protesting, angry black women everywhere they look until some changes are made. I'm tired of being invisible except when the crimes against us or our children are so heinous they make the front page. I'm sick of acting like people who can figure out how to erect multimillion-dollar buildings to house their own offices can't figure out a way to provide safe and sanitary housing for poor black women and their children. I am through with pretending that there are other priorities more important to me than our lives and the lives of our children.

I am, in fact, through with pretending anything. We can't afford the luxury of pretense. We can't allow our fear and insecurity and anger to be things that we only talk about behind closed doors because we don't want to embarrass our black elected officials *in front of the white folks*. As a tactic, being well-behaved just isn't working, so let's try another approach.

Let's bond together as a group with our own specific interests as black women that cross arbitrary lines of economic and social class and join us at the womb. We have to see clearly that we are a unique group, set undeniably apart because of race and sex and with a unique set of challenges as we move toward the twenty-first century. Let's realize that although black men have to deal with racism and white women have to deal with sexism (and white men, hopefully, have to deal with their guilt about all of the evil they have done and continue to do, although I wouldn't count on this), only black women have the dubious distinction of being oppressed by both of the dread "isms."

Let's recognize and reflect upon the meaning of our uniqueness as we face our current crisis. Let's place a value on our children because they are *our children*. All of them. Because the day after a four-year-old Atlanta girlchild was gunned down in her sleep, we should have been there. All of the black women who could get there should have been there to comfort her mother and feed her family and consecrate her memory and promise the little girls she played with in the neighborhood that it will never happen again.

And then we should have marched downtown and asked

the powers that be if they are prepared to work with us to make good on that promise because if they aren't going to cherish and protect our children and our sisters, and make their number-one priority figuring out a way to save our sons and our brothers from becoming the monsters George Bush has always told us they were, then we ought to find somebody who will.

ON REDBONES

There is a poem that begins "The world is too much with us, late and soon." I don't remember what else it says, but I remember those first few lines periodically because they seem to capture for me the true spirit of "world weariness," that overwhelming sense of angst and ennui that signals a complete alienation from what is going on around you. Such a state is usually brought about by an overload of madness that can no longer be processed through your normal channels. The brain and the spirit simply shut down in order to avoid exploding. It's been that kind of month.

I had high hopes for the nineties, I really did. But the decade is only two months old and already I can see that it's going to be a lot more complex than I thought. Notice I use the world "complex," not depressing, crazy, impossible, mind-boggling, overwhelming. My *est*-inclined friends tell me that you have to be careful not to give things more psychic weight than they deserve by describing them in words that neutralize their power to intimidate or distract you. So, "complex" it is. I certainly don't want to be any more distracted or intimidated than I already am. But if I was going to be honest about things, I don't think "complex" does the current madness justice. Saying the first couple of months of 1990 have been "complex" is like saying Mike Tyson is a pretty good boxer. Not only is it inaccurate, it could be dangerous.

But I'm getting ahead of myself. Let me explain . . .

I think it began late last year when I started clipping pictures of black women out of the paper. I was trying to figure out what kind of idea I might have of what black women are if I depended on the media to give me the basic information about who, what, when, where and why. Sort of like wondering what Martians would think if all they knew about Atlanta came to them through the pages of *The Atlanta Constitution*.

So I started clipping out stories about black women from the newspapers and magazines that routinely come through my house. At first it was just an interesting exercise, but very quickly a pattern began to emerge. Black women were conspicuously absent from the newspapers on a daily basis and when we did appear, it was usually looking depressed and distracted while we tried to deal with one of the many complexities of living in public housing communities, or smiling from an old snapshot provided by the family in the hopes of finding us when we disappear from the mall or from our jobs or walking through the neighborhood and are never seen again.

Every once in a while we appeared as the victims of some scam or another or, as the dutifully smiling or crying—as the occasion demands—spouse of some famous black man or another. And in the memorably myopic news coverage of the Marion Barry story, we were prominently featured as the girlfriend-gone-bad who "set up the mayor." (It is interesting to note that Ms. Moore was given credit, or blame, for the set-up by many people, as if the FBI agents in the next room holding her children were just a group of her "play brothers" that she had called to help her take revenge on a philandering lover, but that's not this story.)

The thing is, the picture that was emerging of black women, of me and my sisters, was not a very pleasant one. The complexity of all this began to weigh on me heavily, and then I picked up the paper one morning and I knew it was beyond my feeble abilities to reason and understand.

There on the front page of the morning paper, right below speculation about whether or not Russia was about to undergo a violent change of leadership, was a lengthy article about a black woman who is suing the IRS for back pay and reinstatement of her job as a clerk-typist. The woman claims she was discriminated against by her supervisor, also a black woman, because she is a very light-skinned black person and her supervisor hated and resented her for being a "redbone."

In the course of the trial, the woman testified that her supervisor had said: "You think you're somebody but you're a nobody. You think you're bad but I can do whatever I want to you." The judge, a white male, asked for clarification of the use of the word "bad." After the witness explained, the judge said, "So, to say a musician is bad is to say he's good?" "Yeah," said the witness. "It's slang."

"Complex?" What kind of story is this? How can we hope to understand or appreciate the full ramifications of a case where two black women define their ideas of skin color, using terms well-known in the black community, but totally foreign in the white one? How can a judge who doesn't know the multilayered uses of the term "bad" be expected to understand the complicated historical, cultural and physical information conveyed in the term "redbone"?

Crucial to both sides in this case is the agreement that the plaintiff is, indeed, light complected enough for her skin tone to be a bone of contention. The supervisor, a browner-skinned black woman, has been quoted as saying she didn't consider her accuser light enough to be described as a "red-bone." She went on to say that she put the woman at "medium brown," the range in which she also placed herself.

How can the judge understand the rich variety of skin tones that qualify for "medium brown"? How can he rule on this case without knowing the full ramifications of being described as a "pretty brown-skinned girl"? How can he decide the fate of these two women when he has no understanding of the regional differences that make southern men tend to use the more formal "redbone," while most northern black men cut it to the more familiar "red"? How can he understand the outrage and ambivalence on both sides without hearing my explanation to my daughter when she was three or so when we were walking down M.L. King Jr. Drive and a man tipped his cap and rolled his eyes appreciatively as we passed and said, "What's happnin', Red?" and I answered politely as if he'd called my name?

The answer to all of the above is, of course, the judge can't. There is no way he can make sense of the evidence on either side. The more I thought about this trial and the resulting media coverage, the more I was convinced that "complex" just wasn't enough of a description to capture the true spirit of insanity that permeates the proceedings. So I asked my spiritually advanced friends if I would be asking for trouble if I upgraded my adjective of choice from "complex" to "challenging" and they said they guessed that would be okay. But they had what they thought was a better suggestion for me.

"Stop reading the paper," they said in the soothing voices of those who have traded in their shades for rose-colored glasses. "It will just upset you."

"But how will I know what's going on?" I said.

They smiled again and patted my shoulder gently. "You won't," they said.

"Oh," I said. "I see."

EXCEPTIONAL MEN

*"The Negro race, like all races, is going to be saved by its
exceptional men."*   W.E.B. Dubois

W hen I was a little girl and had just reached the age where
my circle of playmates included more than my cousins
and my sister and the kids on our block, I realized that my
sandy hair, light complexion and undeniably blue eyes were
confusing some of my new friends. Their reactions to this
confusion ran the gamut from bemused eye rolling, to endless questions like, "Are you sure you're not an albino?" to
taunts of being "light, bright and damn near white" or worse,
a white girl who was trying to "get over" by pretending to be
black.

The eye rolling didn't bother me. I answered all questions
easily since I had no confusion about my racial identity. But
the taunting was a little harder to deal with, mostly because
it had a vehement bitterness to it that I had never heard in
other children's voices before. Now it was my turn to be
confused. I consulted my mother.

"Well," she said, "it's like this. When they get mad because they think you're white, it's because of centuries of racism and abuse at the hands of evil white folks. It's an honest and sane response to oppression and one we understand and endorse, right?"

I agreed. Of course, we wanted black folks to be indignant around white folks.

"So, don't take it personally. It's just a case of mistaken identity," my mother said. "Tell them you're black and everything will be fine.

"Now the second one is a little more complicated," my mother continued. "When they are mad at you for being light, they are reacting to the fact that the insanity of American racism makes many people place an increased value on light skin and whiter looking features. It's complete madness," she said with a frown and a shake of her head, "but it means people that look like us sometimes get rewarded for it. And the weak-minded ones sometimes begin to think looking this way makes them better than other black folks. But we're not like that, right?"

Of course we weren't. We had been correctly taught that the reason for our light skin was the enslavement and rape of our great-grandmothers. Anything associated with that rape —light skin, straight hair, blue eyes—was a painful reminder. Pride wasn't even in it.

"So, don't take it personally. Make it clear to them by how you act and what you do that they are your brothers and sisters and you love them, and gradually they will see that you mean it and everything will be fine."

I tell this story here for two reasons. One, to show that I understand the complexity of being part of a racial sub-group that is both punished and rewarded for the genes it shares with its former masters, and two, because my mother was right. Being a light-skinned black American isn't necessarily cause for condemnation, but it must bring with it a recognition that the only way to repay the debt owed for the unearned privilege afforded by the strange circumstances of racism is to understand that to whom much is given, much is expected.

Which brings us to the upcoming Atlanta mayor's race and the two leading contenders, one announced and one unannounced. Both are members of The Privileged Group. Light skinned and keen featured, they are the favored sons of favored families who are already into their third generation of college graduates. Superbly educated and widely traveled, brilliant, hard-working and ambitious, these two black men have been the recipients of every advantage offered to and by their class, and their choice for public service seems in direct response to DuBois's race-saving call to action on the part of exceptional men. In such a race, we, the voters, should be sitting in the catbird seat. We can't miss, except for one problem.

It seems that even though the campaign has just begun officially, there is a real danger that the two candidates may focus on each other instead of on the issues. Instead of a campaign conducted on the highest levels of integrity and creative thought, we may face instead a campaign full of posturing and personalities, personal attacks and private innuendo, demonstrations and counter-demonstrations. We may be forced to consider meaningless exchanges about who lives in the bigger house or the whiter neighborhood and who has spent the most time "visiting" in public housing projects, when in truth, neither one of them has ever lived there.

The point being that it is not their job to pretend to be something they are not. It is their job to figure out what to do for the people who desperately need their help, their commitment and their vision. Because all those good schools and varied experiences and power lunches were supposed to teach them how to be the exceptional men who can lead us by example, inspire us by consistency and dedication and save us from the deadly ills that plague us by showing us a new way. Anything less is just whistling Dixie.

PERSONAL COMMITMENT

I t was a tiny room, jam-packed by the time me and Zeke got there fifteen minutes after the appointed hour. The helmeted police officer directed us to another entrance to the room where we jostled into position with the other people spilling out the door.

I've been a part of enough press conferences like this to know that a lot of those who are there at the start have other appointments, other meetings to go to, other charismatics to staff and serve in whatever capacity the day demands.

The dark suits standing in front of me formed a wall so complete that seeing over, around or between them was clearly going to be a challenge.

But just when I thought I would have to content myself with listening and studying the pin-striped shoulder blades, I glanced through a small space in front of me and there was the Mayor behind an impressive bank of microphones, presiding at a long table crowded with people who seemed to have in common only their discomfort at being there.

There were representatives of the Atlanta City Council, liaisons to the Olympic Committee, spokespersons for the

Atlanta Housing Authority, and leaders of several public housing tenant associations.

And there, seated right next to the Mayor, was the woman who was the true convener of the session, no matter who was allowed to call it to order.

There was Margie Smith, sister-president of the Techwood-Clark Howell Tenant Association and the reason I had ventured into City Hall on a rainy April morning to watch the democratic process at work.

Smith is the elected leader of the tenants of the Techwood housing project, the oldest public housing complex in the nation, which sits on seventy-five acres of prime real estate between Georgia Tech and downtown. Techwood is currently drawing a lot of attention as a possible site for the Olympic Village.

The location is perfect. The money seems to be there to construct suitable temporary shelters for the athletes and it's convenient to a number of proposed Olympic activity sites at Georgia Tech. There is only one problem: People are already living there.

The tenants of Techwood-Clark Howell are almost all women and children. They are almost all black. They are almost all poor. The hard-working people who live in Techwood-Clark Howell almost always find themselves in the position of being discussed and acted upon by people from outside their immediate community. Life-and-death decisions are made and then related to them after the fact when there is little that can be done.

But this time is different. This time, Margie Smith has pulled a chair up to the table and demanded a voice for tenants in *everything* that happens from now on. Period. Which is why she finds herself now sitting beside the Mayor in a room full of people who have serious agendas of their own, speaking for her friends and neighbors in a setting that seems designed to make mere mortals stand in awe of the godlike creatures who find funds to build these amazingly overwrought structures of glass and marble when people are living on the streets.

I am watching Margie Smith from my post behind the blue suits and I remember my own tenure as press secretary at City Hall. I remember how intimidating it can be to talk to this mayor on his own turf. I understand how the microphones and the cameras and bustling staffers with their clipboards and concerned expressions can stifle the words that come so easily in other places.

I know how much thought goes into creating these weird public environments that pretend to embrace honest dissent and open discussion but that in reality only reinforce all the class and gender and racial distinctions that made Margie Smith so mad in the first place.

But now she's listening. Mayor Jackson is outlining a process by which her voice will be heard and her constituents' demands considered. The chairwoman of the Atlanta Housing Authority is assuring her that the authority "does not now have, and has never had" a plan for what will happen to Techwood-Clark Howell vis-à-vis the Olympics, although why that should be reassuring to someone whose destiny the authority holds in its hands is beyond me.

Several other elected officials speak and several appointed officials echo their sentiments. The atmosphere is thick with promises and personal reassurances of good faith, which seem this day to substitute for putting anything in writing.

Questions from Smith and other tenants about who will pick the members of the much-touted advisory committee are smoothed over with pledges of personal concern and sincerity. Demands that tenants be part of a casually mentioned upper-echelon executive decision-making team are greeted with confusion, and finally, the seemingly exasperated Mayor's offer to sign his personal pledge of support "in blood" if the questioner will simply bring him a pin with which to prick his own flesh.

Margie Smith looks weary. She is being overwhelmed by the demands of the form, the necessity for politeness, the presence of police officers to ensure order at all times, the squealing microphones that are placed before her whenever she looks as if she has something to say.

I understand how she feels. Democracy in action is always harder than it sounds in high school civics class, and as I stand there watching Margie Smith, I remember something my father told me about effective use of public meetings.

"The first thing you have to do," he said, "is break the decorum. Kick the table over. Let them know it isn't going to be business as usual."

Once he explained it to me, I understood his conduct at sessions like this one. I appreciated his willingness to raise his voice, to disrespect a system that hadn't even noticed him until he started hollering so loud they couldn't ignore him anymore. I loved his clarity of thought, his passion and his presence of mind in the clinches.

As I stood there listening to the promises for spanking-new day care centers, and multi-use facilities for working parents and elderly people, and increased police presence, *starting tomorrow*, I wished my father was there to say, "How come you couldn't do any of this before I started hollering?"

But I *know* why. Frederick Douglass said that "power concedes nothing without a demand. It never has it never will." And he is right, which is why I was down at City Hall in the first place.

Because I think what Margie Smith is demanding is the right to be treated as a first-class citizen. Because I think that as her sisters we have the responsibility to stand with her when she has to go downtown and convince anybody of the legitimacy of that demand.

I was there because I think those of us who know that finding a way to make black women and children safe and stable in their homes is at least as important as the 'spose-to-be-sacred Olympic Games, have to offer Margie Smith our support, our advice, our counsel and our physical presence when she needs us.

Because it's easier to find your voice in those rooms full of powerful men in dark suits when you have your sister-bankers and sister-administrators there to offer advice and counsel.

It's easier to call a press conference and pack the room when you know you have the backing of your sisters at the Coalition of 100 Black Women. It's easier to write and distribute a press release when you have the expertise of your sisters at the Spelman College Student Government Association.

It's easier to raise the necessary funds to carry on the struggle that will only get more intense as 1996 approaches if you have the backing of your sisters who are members of Delta Sigma Theta or Alpha Kappa Alpha. And I hope it's easier to get the word out when your sister-writers put pen to paper and try to tell the story straight.

And just a friendly word to the Mayor: You don't have to write agreements in blood to prove you are sincere. Simple pen and ink will do just fine.

CLARITY ON CLARENCE

There are questions that seem to be *real* questions, and then there are questions that seem to be beamed in from another galaxy. So obvious are the answers to these questions —when considered by rational women and men—that the tortuous discussions surrounding them take on the surreal air of a Pentagon press briefing by Colin Powell. So many people are paying attention, you start thinking maybe you should too.

Wrong. There is nothing more dangerous than allowing yourself to be sucked into these intergalactic exercises in absurdity. There is nothing to be gained and everything to be lost, including personal sanity and political clarity.

These discussions are certainly not limited to African Americans, but, just between us, we do seem to be particularly susceptible to this kind of weirdness. Most often, our confusion arises when another African American does something that seems so devoid of racial consciousness, so filled with self-hate and self-deception, and so completely outside the flow of our history and culture that we are at a loss to understand or explain his or her actions to ourselves or to each other.

The more bizarre the action of the African American, the more difficult it becomes for us to understand, analyze, justify or explain to ourselves and to each other. In our confusion, we often abandon the hard questions the offending action demands that we ask, and fall back on rhetorical expressions of brotherhood or sisterhood, closing ranks to support the offending African American from those outside our group who may also have found the action in question less than admirable. Our recent history is full of examples of this kind of confusion among us.

Colin Powell's appointment as the head of the Joint Chiefs of Staff made many of us point to him with pride because he was the first African American so designated. The fact that heading up the military arm of one of the most reactionary, repressive, racist governments on the face of the earth is a dubious honor at best for an African American was overlooked in our rush to put Powell's photograph on the front of every African American magazine from *Jet* to *Emerge*. The Martin Luther King Jr. Center for *Non-Violent* Social Change even wanted him to lead its annual march, although he had sense (or political savvy) enough to decline the offer.

Philadelphia Mayor Wilson Goode's bombing of the MOVE houses on Osage Avenue, which resulted in the killing of almost all of the organization's members, including women and children, and the complete leveling of several blocks of African American homes, was justified by many on the basis of the group's "extremism," although, if former Mayor Rizzo had done such a thing, we would have gone berserk.

Our own mayor's recent support of an anti-panhandling ordinance that is clearly aimed at removing homeless black men from the downtown area where they may frighten or offend what the ordinance calls "reasonable people" has not been met with the outcry it deserves because we continue to want to support our brothers in leadership positions, although the same action taken by a white elected official would have been met with screams of racism and demands for programs to help these men recover their lives, not simply remove them from the sunlit benches in Central City Park so that tourists and office workers can have their lunches without having to smell the body odor that is an unavoidable side effect of living outdoors.

But these past incidents pale to insignificance beside the confusion that attends the nomination of Clarence Thomas to the Supreme Court of the United States to replace Brother Justice Thurgood Marshall. Now, it would be difficult for *anyone* to replace Marshall. His unique combination of courage, commitment, intelligence and legal expertise makes him a giant among us. But Clarence Thomas isn't even close. He is wrong on every possible question we can think of that is important to our future survival as a people. He has endeared himself to our enemies—including George Bush—by agreeing to be the point man on all those issues where it confuses things to have a "brother" bring the bad news.

He is wrong on affirmative action, reproductive rights (including a woman's right to a safe and legal abortion), and care of senior citizens. He allows his individual triumph over the poverty of his southern boyhood to be used as a fable to make other black folks think if they just work and study hard, they *too* can be rich and famous and well-fed and beloved of powerful white Republicans.

He is an enemy of our race in particular, and of people of any race in general. So, what's the problem? We should simply recognize another nefarious scheme on the part of the

President to confuse and divide us, follow the lead of Congressman John Lewis, and work for Thomas's overwhelming defeat.

But we aren't doing this. We listen to our "leaders" debate whether or not we are bound to support Thomas simply because he is an African American. We watch them struggle with how to phrase their carefully worded public statements so as not to attack "the brother" since he is "one of our own."

We hear John Jacob, president of the National Urban League, announce his organization's support for Thomas in spite of their feeling that he is simply another conservative voice on an already frighteningly conservative court, and explain the action by saying the President had "checkmated the African American community" with the appointment.

Say what? Nobody can checkmate you unless you agree to play the game they are playing, and I am not now, and have never been, engaged in any game with George Bush and Company. The nomination of Clarence Thomas is not confusing. We should oppose him because he is as wrong as wrong can be and his appointment would be not only devastating to us, but a travesty to the legacy of Thurgood Marshall.

Skin color doesn't qualify anybody to lead us well, serve us effectively or deserve our respect. On the contrary, the fact that Thomas is a brother should make us hold him to an even higher standard, not provide him with a way to weasel out of taking responsibility for being a traitor and an opportunist.

So, next time somebody asks you in a whisper how you feel about Clarence Thomas, don't worry about embarrassing the brother in front of the white folks, or tarnishing the image of a role model somebody else chose for us to admire.

Look them in the eye and tell them you think he's the worst

possible choice for the position, and you hope they'll join you in writing letters to their congressmen and women to oppose his confirmation. *Period.*

Now about that panhandling ordinance . . .

ANTI-SHERO

It's Clarence and Anita's first anniversary and I'm still confused. Not about who said what to whom and why and where and how often. I believe Sister Anita on all details and extend to her my continuing condolences on having had to suffer such lame lines and oppressive behavior from Brother Clarence. What I'm confused about is not the facts, but the *aftermath*. I've been trying for a year and even as I sit looking at the beautiful, back-lit photographs that invariably accompany this latest round of praise-filled articles about her, I still can't understand how Anita Hill became *an African American Shero*.

I have really tried to make sense of it. I have read countless newspaper and magazine articles and even perused a book or two. I appreciate her willingness to speak out on an issue that effects every working woman, but I also know *she was a very reluctant witness* who would have kept silent if the media hadn't forced her hand. I understand the importance of the national dialogue about issues of sexual harassment generated by her testimony, but I also know that *the reason she gave to explain her choice to suffer in silence had to do with wanting to hold onto a job in the Reagan administration.* And I know that the response of the white male senators to her charges energized women across the country to confront their bosses and file complaints and draw lines they'd never drawn before, but I also know that she was already working in the office that was supposed to empower women to do all those things at the very moment she chose personal ambition over making her boss obey the laws they were both sworn to uphold.

So my question a year later is whether being an *unwilling catalyst for change* is the same as being a *conscious change agent.* Does reluctantly agreeing to testify *ten years after the crime was committed* qualify Sister Anita for a permanent place in the pantheon of black warrior women that includes Harriet Tubman and Sojourner Truth and Ida B. Wells and Fannie Lou Hamer and Alice Walker? Isn't this same Sister Anita the woman who made a *choice to work* with the enemies of her race and gender? Not as a double agent, gathering inside information and channelling it to her sisters on the front lines, but as a member of the team. As a well-trained *collaborator.*

Clearly, not everyone is capable, or desirous, of behaving in a manner that can be called *sheroic,* which is not necessarily punishable by being paraded through the streets with shaved head and sack cloth, but certainly must be part of our consideration as we decide how to record Sister Anita's contribution to our common *herstory.*

It is possible to be a very good lawyer, a dedicated public servant, a loving mother, a dutiful daughter, a best-selling novelist or a beauty queen and not be truly *sheroic.* Many women make honorable *individual* choices that nurture their immediate families, earn them college scholarships, secure them well-paying jobs in mainstream America and sustain the affection of their friends and the respect of their neighbors and colleagues. But these choices do not, and should not, earn them a place as *warrior woman of the year and a shining example of how to live life as a free black woman*. That special status must be based on a far more complicated set of qualifications and sacrifices. A true *Shero's* life, although often filled with the contradictions that confirm her humanity, must teach us *by example* and inspire us to continue struggling toward the light.

But this is not the model we find in Sister Anita whose behavior was, and is, a study in individual choices taking precedence over group priorities and needs. After earning her law degree and passing the bar exam, she *voluntarily* took her brain and her energy and her discipline and her creativity and her ambition and put them all to work for a gang of evil-eyed white guys who had seized control of the national government and were busily putting it at the service of their rich, powerful, white-guy friends.

This transition had a demonstrably devastating effect on African American people, women and others deemed unworthy by *the gang*. In addition to the direct cutback of federal programs and funds, the Reagan-Bush administration encouraged a climate of intolerance among right-wing hate groups, anti-abortion activists, cultural imperialists, woman-haters and gay bashers. AIDS was ignored; unemployment was epidemic; L.A. went up in flames and everybody in the White House lied or stonewalled or just forgot whenever anybody started asking too many questions. The twelve Reagan–Bush years were a terrible time of aggressive neglect and violent repression that not only stalled progress but set us back more years than we probably can bear to calculate.

In spite of all this, Sister Anita stuck with the Reagan Republicans and that, too, is her right, as an *individual African American woman* on the Washington fast track. The qualities needed to join that group are simply an above-average intelligence, a driving personal ambition, a willingness to compromise and a strong stomach. Interesting traits, but hardly ones that transform a sister, even a hard working sister, into a certified *Shero*. The *sheroic evaluation process* is of necessity a much different one than any employed by Reagan-Bush and although the criteria may differ slightly from region to region (the West Coast tribes, for example, are usually more inclined toward environmental concerns while the East Coast sisters are focused more on new approaches to urban self-defense) I think we all can agree on the basics: *The Big Five.*

1. *Love of her people.* The *Shero* must be *a Race Woman* and *a Womanist,* dedicated to the survival and advancement of her racial group *overall* and her sisters *specifically.* This does not rule out concern or affection for other individuals or groups. It simply establishes her own racial and gender identity as primary factors in all decisions. This rule requires that the personal be political at every level from choice of mate to source of income and requires a rejection of individualism in favor of the common good.

2. *Commitment to truth.* The *Shero* must not lie directly or through voluntary silence employed to protect personal privilege, avoid unpleasant confrontations or secure individual economic advancement at the price of personal integrity and group empowerment.

3. *Protective of her sisters.* A *Shero* must accept responsibility for the protection of her sisters physically, economically and spiritually. She must identify dangerous individuals, substances and situations clearly as soon as they are known to her so that others will not be at risk.

4. *Courage.* The *Shero* must be courageous enough to confront her enemies when it is right and necessary, trusting her group to protect and sustain her, but not shirking when timely action is required without the kind of immediate support she might have liked.

5. *The long view.* A *Shero* must have confidence in the ability of her group to make a collective commitment to struggle for freedom every minute of every day, each small victory joining with each other small victory until we reclaim our place in the universe as a community of freewomen, freemen, beloved children and honored elders.

Seeing *The Big Five* written down clearly, we can probably agree that the standard is high *but that's the whole point.* Without the highest possible standards, the term *Shero* loses its value as an instrument of empowerment and inspiration. Without absolute clarity about what an *African American Shero* is, and must be, we fall prey to the less-stringent definitions of those outside of our *primary* sisterhood whose agendas may sometimes be complementary to our own, but are never *identical.* As *African American women warriors*, we must reserve the right to evaluate Sister Anita against the yardstick of our own unbroken legacy of black female struggle and then come to our own conclusions.

And when we do, *she is found wanting.* She is found compromising and confusing the issue. She is found silent and suppressed, adrift in a white male world where Ronald Reagan and Oral Roberts signed her checks and Judge Bork was a personal hero. Far from the steadying embrace of her sisters, she is found standing alone at the crossroads, trying to renegotiate her deal with the Devil simply because he's demanding his penance in public, *as the Devil is wont to do,* even when we'd prefer to keep things under wraps.

Which makes Sister Anita pretty much like the rest of us, living our small individual lives, being used by history without being *changed* by it, stumbling along our solitary paths without ever really knowing the strength of sisterhood and the exhilaration of having nothing to hide. Nothing to be ashamed of, if that's what you're willing to settle for, but not enough to leave her enshrined by default in the company of our *true Sheroes*, with whom we placed her in the heat of the moment, but where she clearly doesn't belong any more than Clarence belongs on the Court.

And if all this still sounds a little harsh, considering what the sister's been through, *just try to imagine Fannie Lou Hamer working for the Reagan Administration . . .*

FATAL FLOOZIES

I'm sure Madonna didn't do her sex *book* to help people understand Magic Johnson's sex *life*, but it does. I recommend it highly to those who are having a difficult time squaring the image they have of Magic with his recent revelations. Read the text. Study the pictures. The book is a tribute to the powerful mystery of human beings *fucking*, and the seemingly endless ways they find to do it. No matter what your reaction to the specific sexual things Madonna has chosen to explore, her book proves beyond a shadow of a doubt that there's a whole lot of sexual stuff going on out there that never showed up on "The Cosby Show" and upon which repressive legislation, health concerns and moral outrage usually have no effect at all.

Admittedly overpriced and certainly overhyped, the book completed a thought that began for me with viewing Robert Mapplethorpe's photograph of gay men in dog collars urinating in each other's wide open mouths. *Okay*, I said mentally to Mapplethorpe. *You win. I don't get a vote on any of this. Some stuff is nobody else's business. It's personal.* Magic Johnson already knew this.

My friends didn't see it that way. Their reactions were overwhelmingly negative. My attempts to discuss the book's significance as a valuable addition to the frank, non-judgmental public discussion of human sexuality that will have to precede any truly effective AIDS education and pre-vention programs were met with derisive hoots and a fast flip to one photo or another meant to provide irrefutable proof that Madonna was *"nothing but a hoe"* and that the people she had photographed were some weird, perverted beings whose sexual practices and problems were no more a threat to us *normals* than the mating habits of poisonous snakes. This leap of ignorance allowing for the necessary divisions into *us* and *them*, the hooter had the mental hedge needed to keep on thinking safe sex is only a necessary precaution if you're having sex with *fags* and *freaks*.

I had already retired *Sex* from my coffee table when Magic Johnson reentered basketball, reretired from it, published his autobiography and appeared on live television for the first time with his wife Cookie and their infant son. There he was on "The Oprah Winfrey Show," discussing in graphic detail his highly pleasurable but ultimately deadly sex life. He ex-plained his frankness by saying he wanted young people to understand how he got the virus so they could better protect themselves from it.

How wonderful, I thought. *An unassailable reason if there ever was one.* His admission that he had the virus had proven once and for all that nice guys/strong guys/famous guys with great smiles and beautiful wives and money in the bank *can get it*. Now, through his willingness to speak openly and without shame about his sex life, he's going to make the critical dis-tinction between being sorry he got sick and sorry he had a lot of exciting, voluntary, non-traditional sex. *Bravo*, I thought.

Magic continued to be relaxed and forthcoming when he

was joined on the set by his smiling wife. I was impressed with her serenity as he held her hand and described the extensive premarital sexual experimentation that would have labelled him a *"serious freak"* in any black community I've ever known. But then Oprah was moved to ask if discussing the topic made her feel uncomfortable and Mrs. Johnson shook her beautiful head. "It didn't bother me as long as I got my respect," she said. "As long as I was never treated like a *floozie* or whatever, I could deal with it."

Oprah nodded and turned to confirm with Magic that this was indeed what these other women were: *floozies.* "That is correct," he said. "That is correct." Oprah squeezed Cookie's free hand reassuringly and they moved on, but I was stuck.

Floozies? What century were they living in? I hadn't heard the word in years and suddenly these three wealthy, famous, well-traveled, articulate black people threw it out casually in what was otherwise a fairly sophisticated discussion of life and love in *the plague years.* They assumed we were all in agreement about what constituted a *floozie* and on the un-desirability of being one. No further definitions seemed nec-essary to them, *but I needed clarification.* Were they *floozies* because they had sex with lots of men or because *he* had sex with lots of women? How many constitutes a *lot?* How many is *too* many? Does it count as heavily against you if you have sex in the missionary position and promise not to laugh out loud no matter how good it feels?

I was, of course, familiar with the word. Everybody knows what *floozies* are. Their many unacceptable behaviors are outlined to young girls at puberty, along with the rigid rules governing every aspect of sexual exchange. Since only strict adherence to these rules guaranteed the safety and respect afforded *good girls*, we were expected to have a clear under-standing and working knowledge of *floozie* behavior. This information was passed from woman to woman with great seriousness and an understanding that if you had any objections you were to declare them up front rather than claiming ignorance later. Deviation required permission in advance.

The behaviors that identify a *floozie* have remained fairly constant since my girlhood, stubbornly refusing to admit to such historic change-agents as the pill, the sixties and the sexual revolution. I repeat them here for those who have forgotten the basics.

You are a *floozie* if you:
1. have sex with men other than your steady boyfriend, fiancé, husband or significant other;
2. have sex with men strictly for pleasure;
3. have sex with men on the first date;
4. have sex with men who are committed to others;
5. have sex with more than one man on the same day;
6. have sex with more than one person at the same time;
7. have sex with more than ten men from the time you become sexually active until the time you mate for life or become celibate;
8. have sex with people watching;
9. watch people have sex;
10. have sex for money or as an acknowledged trade-off for expensive gifts, backstage passes and front row seats.

Breaking one of the rules was considered the first step on the road to ruin. Breaking two was considered a clear indication of bad character. Breaking three showed a lack of discipline and poor judgment and four down indicated an almost irreversible slide into the pit. Breaking five or more of the rules was all the evidence necessary to designate someone a *practicing floozie* with no place in the rigidly righteous sister-hood of good girls and monogamous women.

This list never bothered me growing up. I did not intend to incur the wrath of my family and the scorn of my friends by becoming a *floozie* and I couldn't imagine doing most of the stuff on the list anyway although I did an average amount of high school necking and enough passionate petting to make me appreciate fully consummated sexual intercourse when I first experienced it with my steady in a Washington, D.C., Holiday Inn. *But I had followed the rules.* I didn't actu-ally have sex until my beau and I had agreed to marry and I was absolutely convinced that we would stay together always, joined by mutual respect and ironclad monogamy.

When we broke up two years later, I remember hoping he was wrong when he shouted at me that I'd never find a decent husband since I was "nothing but used goods." After all, it was 1967 and virginity had always been a part of the status assessment process, but I had had only one lover and he was my announced fiancé at the time of our coupling. I was still a long way from being a *floozie.* So, I indulged my curiosity and had two very pleasurable one night stands with two old friends who were delighted at this unexpected turn of events and then I got engaged again and was married a few months later. At this point, *the floozie factor* ceased to be a reality in my life. I was happily married and expected to remain that way for the duration. *I was twenty.*

Ten years later, I was divorced, had a five-year-old daugh-ter, my first apartment ever, a feminist friend, a good paying part-time job and a joint custody arrangement that left me childfree for five days every two weeks. I had an eclectic circle of men friends and colleagues about whom I'd been sexually curious for years. I had no desire to remarry, no need of financial assistance and no respect for traditional monogamy, which I now viewed as the death of love. Armed with the classic bohemian belief in the truth of pure experience, *and an absolute commitment to birth control*, I set out consciously to explore the full range of my sexuality as part of my overall development of myself as a free woman.

During the highly charged period that followed, I explored the realm of my own sexual powers through a series of liaisons with men that I chose because they were wonderful writers or political comrades or interesting dinner partners or had all the best music or knew how to do something physical that made me feel good or made me laugh or listened well or gave me a shoulder to cry on at a weak moment when I just wanted to be held close by somebody.

I gave myself permission to try whatever I could think of *with one man at a time.* Short ones, tall ones, rich ones, poor ones, boring assholes and beautiful bisexuals. Sometimes I'd learn a lot about my body and my spirit and my limits and sometimes I'd just have fun and go home alone so I could wake up in my own bed and start writing early.

I was *a responsible, sexually active woman* and in the process of my personal explorations, I broke five of the ten rules on the *floozie* alert list. I always had good explanations for these breeches of etiquette, but the simple truth of the matter is that most of the time I was engaged in the individual pursuit of sensual adventure. The men I was seducing, and the ones who were seducing me, had all agreed to a voluntary contract based not on conversation and commitment, but on sexual pleasure and discretion.

I didn't feel like a *floozie*. I still did all the things I usually did. I went to work, picked my daughter up at school, cooked dinner for friends, went to the movies and marched in political demonstrations. I was living my life the way I wanted to and I felt like a free woman, *just like Magic felt like a free man.* And he was, and we all liked him, and we still do, which is why we are so willing to sacrifice the humanity of his partners and allow them to be called *floozies* so he can still be our innocently smiling hero. We want him to be the innocent victim of some anonymous *fast girls* because the fantasy of the *fatal floozies* helps us feel safer, just like we used to when we were pretending the only people who got AIDS were gay white men.

So I'm hoping that next time the question comes up, Magic will have had a chance to think about it a little harder and when Oprah asks him about *floozies*, he'll say: "'Well, Oprah, the truth is, I don't like to use the word *floozies*. My partners were all sexually active, adult women who enjoyed having sex with me and with other professional athletes and entertainers. I shared a lot of sexual pleasure and a lot of laughs with these women during a wonderful, exciting time in my life. Of course, if I had known I might die or endanger others from indulging my sexual curiosity, I would have done things differently. I was ignorant and so were they. But I'm not going to blame them and call them *floozies* now because they freely shared themselves with me and I freely shared myself with them. I'm just sorry I didn't have better information for my sake and for theirs. That part of my life is over now, but I wish those women continued good health and long life and the blessing of finding a person who will cherish them the way I cherish my wife. Thanks for letting me clarify that, Oprah. *Shall we move on?*"

Here's hoping.

BEVERLY'S BOOTS

Sisterhood is a funny thing. It's easy to recognize, but hard to define. It's an embracing circle and a 100-yard dash. It's as familiar as a favorite pair of sneakers and as mysterious as a cat's-eye stone. It is a lifeline to the future and a tangible link to the past. It's easier to say what it *feels* like than to say what it *is*. It's also safer to be as specific as possible. Last month is as good a place to start as any.

Now I know March was supposed to come in like a lion and go out like a lamb, but nothing prepared me for what happened in between the two. It started off like any other month. Bills to pay. Groceries to buy. Midterms to monitor. But somewhere near the end of the second week I got a notice telling me that Spelman College was hosting a speakers' series featuring *Essence* Editor Susan Taylor, writer and scholar Mary Helen Washington and poet Nikki Giovanni. Around the same time, Sister Sue Ross, Atlanta documentary photographer extraordinaire, invited me to a fiftieth birthday party for writer Toni Cade Bambara at The Hammonds House, the vibrant West End cultural center that had just celebrated its own first birthday.

I was delighted and I tacked the invitations to my bulletin board, savoring the sight of them as if they were Sunday School sweets. I was ready to be immersed in sisterhood; surrounded by sisterhood; consumed by sisterhood! It had, after all, been a long, hard winter. The election of George Bush and Dan Quayle, after a seemingly endless campaign, had filled D.C. with the same crowd of evilly posturing white men who had been in charge for the last eight years. The election had depressed me more than I expected it to. I felt adrift, frightened, marooned in a country that was making it clear with depressing regularity that it had little interest in, or time for, me and mine.

I saw the same confused look in the eyes of many of my sisters, and I became aware of our unspoken but undeniable movement inward. Looking out was a little too dangerous right now, and in all the confusion, it was getting harder and harder to feel like anything we did made any difference. I felt like we should all start wearing whatever camouflage we could find and hunker down to wait out the storm.

But in the Spelman invitation to a week rich in *sisterspeak*, and in the joyful celebration that I had no doubt would greet Toni's birthday, I saw an antidote, however temporary, to the Bush-Quayle blues. Help, as they say, was on the way, and I was more than ready for it.

What I wasn't ready for was my reaction to that concentrated dose of sisterhood. I didn't know how hungry I was for a dose of black female reality. Within a space of four days, I listened to Mary Helen Washington talk about the triumphant struggles of black foremothers, and I was inspired by her scholarship and her energy. I heard Susan Taylor make all the right connections between our lack of group identity and our group's current problems, and I was energized by her commitment. I felt Nikki Giovanni's wildly individual spirit on the campus, and I laughed at her continuing outspoken specificity. I stood in a circle of black women in Spelman President Johnnetta Cole's campus living room listening to writer Sonia Sanchez invoke the blessings of whatever gods and goddesses may be for our private and collective journeys, and I felt comforted and loved and challenged and strong. And I stood in a crowded room and cheered the triumphant genius of sisterwriter Toni Cade Bambara, and I wept and laughed and wondered if I was finally losing my mind for real. Presidential politics aside, I cautioned myself, you're out of control, a dangerous stage for a black woman in America. Was I crazy, I wondered, to be feeling this free? Was I forgetting who was really in charge? All of a sudden, I felt my blues coming back strong and that's when I saw Beverly's boots.

Right there in the middle of the party, in the midst of the sisters serving fried potatoes and caviar and the brothers trying to navigate the intricacies of being outnumbered 25 to 1 in a room full of strong black women, Beverly was wearing a pair of wildly fringed cowboy boots. They were silver and black or silver and white—I don't remember. What I do remember is that they were funny and outrageous and silly and stylish and absolutely free. Those boots didn't give a damn about George Bush. They were too busy studying. They refused to even acknowledge Dan Quayle. They were too busy planning. And they didn't even know the meaning of the word cynical. They were too busy dancing.

And suddenly, I stopped worrying. About the Big Boys in D.C. About the home boys in Atlanta. About insanity and politics and things that go bump in the night. I looked at Beverly's boots, and I understood that nothing they do means we can't go out and celebrate our existence and confirm our struggles and evaluate our progress and believe in our future and laugh together at our continuing survival and wear our cowboy boots whenever we please.

So thanks, Beverly and Toni and Mary Helen and Sonia and Johnnetta and Susan and Wild Nikki. I needed that. I think I've got a trip to the shoe store coming.

PART THREE

FORGETTING

TO

FUSS

BLAMING THE VICTIM

The months before my mother died were the worst ones of my life. I was powerless to stop the cancer that was eating her alive. My marriage of ten years was shuddering to a halt. I was working at a job I hated and wondering if I would ever have enough faith in myself as a writer to quit and get on with my Real Work. I was broke most of the time, scared all of the time, alienated from my friends, astonished at my enemies, and exhausted.

Most of what I remember about that time is going to work in a daze, trying to reassure my daughter that everything was going to be okay (even though I didn't believe it for a second) and drinking. Pernod, a sickly yellow, licorice-tasting liquor that is usually found in French films, was my anesthetic of choice. I would like to say I drank it because I liked the taste, or because it made me draw upon my Paris fantasies for strength and sustenance, but both of those would be lies. I drank Pernod because it got me drunk. Fast.

At first I mixed it with water like the label suggested, but after awhile, I didn't bother. I'd throw a couple of ice cubes in and let them provide whatever mixer was required. It wasn't about taste. It was about retreat. About forgetting.

My alone-again apartment had only one small bedroom where my daughter slept. I camped out on the sofa bed in the living room. That's not really accurate, I almost never bothered to pull the bed out. It wasn't necessary. I usually slept in my clothes anyway. I would turn out all the lights, stare out at the glowing Atlanta skyline and start drinking.

It usually took me four or five hours to get drunk enough to fall asleep. Sometimes less, depending on how strong I could stand the drinks. Most of the time, I'd be out by midnight, which suited me just fine. Pernod guaranteed me dreamless if fitful sleep, and a temporary respite from the clanging and keening that was going on inside my head.

I went on like this for three or four months, and gradually I was able to allow myself to think a little before I started drinking. And then, a little more, and then, a little more. And gradually, as I got a grip on my new life, I didn't need the Pernod at all. The darkness and the quiet and the glowing lights of other people's dreams were soothing enough to allow me to let the demons out where I could see them, confront them and finally beat them back into submission.

But I was lucky. I had a child who loves me. I had friends who never stopped offering sympathetic shoulders to cry on. I had my Real Work which was beginning to show itself in spite of my efforts to hold it at bay.

I also had a clean, safe apartment, a closet full of warm clothes, a car that I could usually afford to put gas in and, if all else failed, a family that would have taken me in if I had had to ask them to. But those few months showed me something about despair I hadn't understood before. Those months made me understand that it is possible to find the life you're living so incomprehensibly terrible that any alternative seems preferable, even the ones you know aren't good for you. Good health is only of concern to those who want to live.

I don't spend a lot of time thinking about those days, but they came back to me in a rush last week when I read some recently released statistics that showed the widening gap between white and black life expectancy. It was a small article in last month's paper, tucked away somewhere off the front page, and it told me that a white child born today has a good chance of living to be 75.6 years old. A black baby can only expect 69.4, down three years from 1984 and fading fast.

The researchers went on to say that furthermore, black people are not dying primarily because of the diseases that ravage all Americans—cancer, heart disease and stroke. We are dying instead of AIDS (usually the result of unsafe sex and the sharing of drug paraphernalia), drug overdoses, homicides, accidents usually involving drunk driving and chronic liver disease due to alcohol abuse.

"This is essentially self-destructive behavior," they explained. "It is a pattern you get when people are in despair."

That's the part that made me remember those months of solitary drinking. I closed my eyes and saw the pattern I had slipped into temporarily repeating itself with depressing regularity in black households across the country. Black people —hopeless, homeless, jobless, leaderless—trying to drink away or smoke away the reality of our terribleness. I understood the need to escape reality by any means necessary. I also understood that my few months of solitary desperation in no way compare to what it must feel like to live on the street, eat whatever you can scrounge and hope like hell for a mild winter.

I've been trying to write about all this for three days, and somehow I don't think I'm any closer now to what I want to say than I was all those words and all those revisions ago. I think what bothers me is that calling this completely under-standable behavior "self-destructive" denies the fact that it is occurring in response to a society that has written most of us off as excess baggage. Such ingenuous denials ignore the inability of the human spirit to continue to thrive when all roads are dead-ends and keeping hope alive an impossible dream. Such a label seems perilously close to blaming the victim and denies us even the dignity of death by our own subconscious hand rather than waiting for whichever method *They* finally decide on, depending on who's in charge when it's time for the final solution.

Now don't misunderstand me. I don't endorse or applaud our collective suicide pact, but I understand it and I think it's as honorable a choice as pretending to bask in the glow of those thousand points of imaginary light. The problem, after all, didn't start with the purchase of a bottle of Thunderbird or a hit of crack cocaine. It started with the docking of the first slave ship and all the horrors that came after.

Blaming us now for refusing to go on with the charade and deciding to check out early only adds insult to injury. And pretending not to understand *why* is only another manifesta-tion of the unspoken conviction that slaves and their de-scendants aren't supposed to feel complex emotions like despair or love or rage or desperation and then act upon them with whatever means are at hand. But we've got better infor-mation than that. And so do They.

RECYCLING BLUES

M y kitchen has changed. Although never a model of domestic organization, I have always managed to hold complete chaos at bay by refusing to let a sink full of dirty dishes sit around overnight, by tossing out any leftovers I can't identify by basic food group and original date of presentation, and by taking out garbage and trash regularly. (Especially discarded raw chicken innards ever since I made the tragic mistake of tossing some casually in with the garbage one hot summer night and woke up the next morning to find my entire house in the grip of an evil smell I won't even try to describe, but which I promised myself I would never encounter again if I could possibly help it.)

But now everything has changed. The corner by the back door is crowded with bags of aluminum cans, boxes of glass containers and stacks of days-old newspapers. In order to use this door for entrances and exits—or even to crack it just a little to let the breeze blow in between the burglar bars—one must bear the consequences that are the result of any movement of the intricately arranged piles. And to what is this new kitchen complexity attributable? I am, with the zeal of the recently converted, *recycling*.

My family, immediate and extended, thinks it's funny. They roll their eyes at each other when Freddie the Flower Child on "A Different World" launches into a harangue about the planet being in peril. They chuckle audibly when they hear the glass containers clanging in the trunk when I'm on my way to the recycling bins—which as far as I can tell are all located at least a fifteen-minute ride away from my all-black neighborhood. They grumble when it's their turn to do the dishes and the sink is full of bottles that must be rinsed and de-labeled before they are ready to hit the recycling bin.

At first, they thought it was just a phase I was going through. Some kind of misplaced, middle-aged idealism. I have, after all, never been known for my interest in saving the planet. I don't have anything *against* the planet, of course. Some of my best friends are Earthlings, but my immediate *personal* concerns run more toward fighting racism and sexism. There are, after all, only so many hours in any given day, and I spend so much time fussing and fighting back now that I barely have time left over to hang out with my daughter and shampoo my true love's dreadlocks.

So when I rescued an empty Andre's bottle from the waste basket and scraped off the gold foil around the neck to ready it for recycling, my friends laughed at me. "You're recycling *Andre's* bottles now?" they said.

"If you all would bring me Dom Perignon, I'd recycle Dom Perignon bottles," I said with the slightly self-righteous confidence of the newly correct, amused at the class distinctions that made Andre's champagne bottles seem to them less desirable as fodder for the recycling bin than the higher-priced bubblies.

Although my smug feelings of super-correctness carried me through the first few weeks of my new environmental efforts, I will admit that after awhile my enthusiasm started to fade. I looked at the bulging bags and overflowing boxes stacked accusingly at my back door and I tried to remember what had started me on this path in the first place. I think it was Alice Walker.

Living in the peace and serenity of the northern California woods, Sister Alice has more time to appreciate the beauty of the natural environment than I do during my daily treks through downtown Atlanta. Her concern for the sea, for the animals and for the air began to creep into her work more and more until she finally published a book of new and collected poems called *Her Blue Body Everything We Know: Earthling Poems, 1965–1990.*

The "her" of the blue body is the earth, which, according to the astronauts, looks like a big blue marble from a distance. The "Earthlings" are all of us who live and die on the fragile surface of the marble and who, according to Sister Alice and others, are messing things up with the kind of unconcern we usually reserve for conquering Third World nations who think they have a right to run their own affairs.

Shame, says Sister Alice, who doesn't tend to have much of a sense of humor about such things. We ought to *know* and *do* better.

Okay, I thought, but what can I do? I'm from Detroit where recycling meant stripping a car before you took it to the junk yard. The question led me to my local bookstore where I found a book called *50 Simple Things You Can Do to Save the Earth.* It was a little book, published by The Earthworks Press in Berkeley, California, and it sells for $5. It seemed pretty straightforward and non-mystical, its northern California roots notwithstanding, and I took it home to see what might work for me.

I already knew there were some things I wasn't prepared to do yet, like give up the long, hot showers that sometimes seem to be the only way to make my brain wake up and start writing. I also knew there were some things that just didn't apply to me *personally* anymore, like the question of cloth diapers or disposables. But I did find some things in that little book I could do easily, and which I think would please Sister Alice.

Things like snipping the plastic rings on six-packs of sodas and beer so they don't make their way to the ocean and choke unsuspecting marine life. Things like drinking my coffee out of washable mugs rather than Styrofoam cups that stay around for 500 years or so after we toss them out. Things like eating less beef and more vegetables. Things like taking my old newspapers and empty glass containers to the recycling bin so they can be melted and shredded and used again.

Things like collecting aluminum cans and either taking them to the recycling centers myself or hanging them on the dumpsters where I know the brothers come searching on a regular basis. (The first time you watch a brother who is used to having to pick through all the garbage in the dumpster to find cans realize that somebody has already bagged a couple of pounds of them and left them hanging in easy reach, you will never toss a can casually in with the general trash again.)

There's a lot of other things in the book I haven't gotten to yet, but I hope I will be able to sustain my focus long enough to try some more of them. I'd like to get some of those reusable macrame grocery bags that you take to the store yourself and that look so northern California hip to me. I'd like to plant a tree or two, although I'm famous for killing even the heartiest house plant with my overzealous watering.

But for right now, I'm just trying to get the basics to become a part of my regular routine. And so far, so good. Last week, I even broke down and decided to get a couple of real containers for my haphazard piles to neaten up my kitchen corner as soon as I can find some that are ecologically correct and not made of environmentally evil plastic.

And even though my friends continue to roll their eyes when they see me rinsing out an Andre's bottle or two after a long weekend, they have learned to keep their opinions to themselves. Even if they won't give me the satisfaction of admitting it, they know we're going to have to breathe this air and depend on these oceans and use these trees just like those upper-middle-class white environmentalists who most of us tune out even when they're making sense.

Crack and AIDS and unemployment and homelessness are definitely plagues we have to fight against, but so is the individually preventable pollution that is strangling our planet before our eyes.

After all, *her blue body everything we know.*

FIGHTING MONSTERS

I have a confession to make. I did not vote in the Georgia primary. There. It's out. I've said it in print, and I can't take it back. I've had a month to feel guilty about it, and my grandmother said confession is good for the soul, so there it is. *I confess.*

I tried to vote. I even drove to my polling place, but I didn't go in. I circled the place twice and then slunk off, hoping nobody had seen me. It was my own fault. Well, not *fault* really. My own *choice*. I *decided* not to vote. Me. The person who goes early to the polls and parades around for the rest of the day wearing that self-righteous little sticker that tells the world: *I voted. Did you?*

I am a true child of the sixties, and I believe those *please register* slogans about people dying for my right to vote. I saw them do it. Plus, I have always been infatuated with the *idea* of Democracy. Of people picking someone from their ranks to lead them. Of encouraging discussion and debate and then letting the voters decide.

I was always excited by my own participation in the process, the sweet symmetry of standing in line with my small daughter, waiting to cast a vote when I can remember standing in line with my own exhausted mother so she could vote before going home to fix dinner.

And I have voted for all kinds of reasons. I have voted because I was excited about a candidate and thought she/he would do a good job. I have voted because I was angry at an incumbent and wanted him/her out of office. I have voted because I wanted to stop a war or support a movement or make a change. And sometimes I have voted because I think that's what good citizens are supposed to do as part of their responsibility to their country.

But this time was different. This time I couldn't find any reason to vote at all. Who was I going to vote for? Among the white male/white shirt/dark suit/power tie candidates whose names were on the ballot, in whom should I place my black nationalist/feminist/artist trust? Who among these painfully smiling white men really cares about me and my sisters?

Which of these candidates has ever seen the black women who parade past my door all day long on their way to find the crack man? Who among these wealthy white men understands what it means to be a fifteen-year-old pregnant teenager who can't read, already has one baby, and just discovered her boyfriend is HIV positive?

Who among these men can understand not being able to ask your doctor for abortion information because part of the money that pays the light bill at the clinic comes from a federal grant? Which of them has comforted a terrified friend with breast cancer and no health insurance?

I listened to their interviews and I watched their debate, and I couldn't tell the difference between them no matter how hard I tried. When election day rolled around, the process itself seemed to be so corrupt and filled with deceit that my participation would be an endorsement of everything I am struggling against.

So what to do? I can't drop out of the process altogether. This was a *primary*, so my vote would have been part of the internal decision-making among the Democrats. *Next time*, a no-show gives a vote to George Bush or Pat Buchannan, and that level of guilt I'm not prepared to accept.

But I'm at a loss as to my options. I never did learn to make Molotov cocktails, and I still believe in the *idea* of the process enough so that I don't want to move to the country and grow my own food and bake my own bread and let the rest of the world go for broke.

But maybe that's not such a bad idea. Ever since I circled my polling place twice and couldn't make myself park and go in, I keep thinking about a quote I read once from Nietzsche, the philosopher:

> Whoever fights monsters should see to it that in the process he does not become a monster. And when you look long into the abyss, the abyss also looks into you.

I think maybe the primary was a little too close to the abyss for me. After all, nobody died for my right to be a monster.

FORGETTING TO FUSS

There are lessons that, at almost middle-aged, I thought I had already learned well enough not to have to repeat. Things like the impossibility of passion without freedom, the futility of unrequited love and the inappropriateness of patriotism, but I guess I was wrong because here I am again, after all these years, eyes glued to an ecstatically waving white man with a full head of hair and a strange accent. Here I am again; nodding, smiling, believing, singing along: *"Don't stop thinking about tomorrow."*

I remember the moment I first felt what I can now identify as patriotic fervor. I was thirteen and the only president I knew was Dwight D. Eisenhower, who my parents regarded with the despairing contempt black intellectuals reserve for powerful white men who aren't very bright. My parents had followed the Nixon–Kennedy race closely and their satisfaction at the Democratic victory was obvious, but tempered, as always, by an unshakable belief in the inability of any white man to do right by Negroes over the long haul, especially a politician.

My parents celebrated the possibilities for *Negro advance-*

ment under the new President, but the famed Kennedy wit, charm and good looks cut no ice at our house. The much ballyhooed beauty of the new First Lady was greeted with a contemptuous snort and a few fast comparisons to Dorothy Dandridge and Lena Horne in which Jackie K. was found wanting. This was white politics, after all. We had to participate, but we didn't have to care about their kids.

All of which was fine by me. The Kennedy campaign had simply been part of the constant hum of political activity and analysis that was always part of the background noise in our house. I was much more concerned about starting the ninth grade at a new school than about the new presidency. So when I sat down on Inauguration Day to watch the proceedings, I was unprepared for the intensity of my emotional reaction.

I don't remember exactly what touched it off, although I do recall being disproportionately moved by Kennedy's sincere attempts to use his top hat to keep the sun's glare off of Robert Frost's manuscript so Frost's old eyes could make out his own words and he could finish reading his poem, but I attributed that to the fact that my mother loved his work and used to recite "Stopping by Woods on a Snowy Evening" to my sister and me at bedtime almost as often as she read Langston Hughes.

I don't recall being smitten with his good looks or especially impressed by his youth. Back then, early forties was still pretty old to me. I do remember initially being distracted by his accent, but at what point the accent faded away and I was able to decipher the dream, I can't say. All I know is that by the time he gotta "ask not what your country can do for you . . ." I was a believer.

I realize, of course, that I was not the only one. All over the country, people were being energized, but I had not been raised to behave this way. My world view was shaped by people who saw our collective relationship to this country through the prism of slavery. They channelled their normal, human desire for group identity into race pride and a defiant pan-Africanism that embraced the whole continent since questions of specific tribal affiliation were rendered moot by The Middle Passage. American citizenship was regarded as an unworthy goal for *thinking* black people.

In elementary school, I refused to say the Pledge of Allegiance to the Flag because it contained lines like ". . . with liberty and justice for all . . ." and I knew Negroes were walking in protest all over Montgomery, Alabama, rather than riding on segregated buses.

In high school, I refused to stand for the singing of the National Anthem because I wasn't going to be caught crooning about ". . . the land of the free and the home of the brave . . ." when black churches were being bombed in Birmingham and little girls my own age were dying on a pre–Sunday school dash to the downstairs bathroom.

White America had made it clear that we were not welcome here and if they didn't want us to be Americans, we returned the feeling double. Love of country was an emotion circumstances had conspired to deny us. *And so be it.*

The problem is that this is an *intellectual position*, developed after years of discussion and analysis. Pure patriotism is an emotional experience, an involuntary, deeply nationalistic feeling rendering one temporarily colorless, genderless, classless and connected by common land and blood memories to the totality of your kinswomen and men.

As if I had learned nothing from all those nights of lively debate around the dinner table, I sat listening to President Kennedy and feeling for the first time a connection between my small, west side of Detroit black female self and my *fellow Americans.* I wanted to join forces with other American citizens who suddenly felt as close to me as my first cousins.

I wanted to help this man transform the country from the racist, sexist, mean-spirited place it previously had shown itself to be into a place that could really feel like *home*. I knew I had to act on this feeling to make it real. This was something new and powerful and comforting in a way I couldn't really articulate yet, but didn't want to lose in the meantime. *I decided to join the Peace Corps.*

My plan was to finish high school, enlist and then start college when my tour of duty was over. Brimming with confidence and commitment, I outlined the plan to my mother who was grading a bad batch of fourth-grade spelling tests on the kitchen table. She listened to me and then shook her head as if I had just announced my intention to move to Chicago and pass for white.

"We're Negroes," she said, as if I must have forgotten this critical fact in the sudden flush of my newfound patriotism. "We don't have to go anywhere to find somebody who needs help. All we have to do is walk out the front door."

This was not the reaction I expected from a woman who once told me that when Franklin Roosevelt died she felt like she'd lost a member of her family. She must have seen my surprise and she patted my arm sympathetically before turning back to her work. "The Peace Corps is not for us," she said. "Don't let that white man distract you from what we have to do a little closer to home."

A little closer to home? Couldn't she see that joining a national movement and being sent abroad as part of a force for international good will was a lot more exciting than picketing our all black neighborhood's only supermarket because they sold us rotten meat and spoiled vegetables? Didn't she know that teaching reading to people who didn't dream in English would be much more romantic than her own unending labors at an inner city elementary school where half the kids came to class in the morning hungry and hostile?

Couldn't helping my country ultimately be good for Negroes too?

All good questions, and certainly worthy of sustained consideration by an idealistic thirteen year old, and I did consider them, along with equally deserving questions like, what really makes a girl fast, and how do people kiss with their mouths open, and what is the appropriate response when somebody at school asks me if I'm an albino because they've never seen a black person as light as I am, *especially not with no blue eyes!*

But then the assassinations changed almost everything, and Vietnam changed the rest, and suddenly the idea of putting my faith in any leader seemed a fairly risky business, even if he was a charismatic white man from a wealthy family with underworld connections. My mother's words were beginning to make more sense to me. I figured I better leave white folks' business alone and concentrate on some things where clarity was still possible.

Besides, the store in my neighborhood was still selling bad meat and calling it a bargain. The Detroit police were still shooting black civilians in the back on a regular basis and the auto factories were starting to lay off people who were never going to work again, *anywhere*, although we didn't know that yet.

But now it's election night, thirty years later, and I sit listening to Bill Clinton, virtually voiceless from the endless campaign, croaking out his vision for a new America, calling on the rest of us to pitch in and help; *to be Americans again!* and I want to be part of it! My mind is already busily cataloging the skills I possess that could be put in the service of *my country*. I watch Bill Clinton smiling happily and waving from the steps of the Arkansas State House and I am thirteen years old again, ready to sign on and sign up and deliver myself to the door of the White House as a volunteer in service to this grinning Great White Hope who likes Fleetwood Mac, smoked a little dope, demonstrated against the war and has an alter ego that plays "Heartbreak Hotel" on the saxophone.

Which is why I stopped watching long enough to light some incense and look away for a few minutes. I know I've got to be careful. Any white man who can distract me from my long-term goal of trying to overthrow the existing order and seize control for African American Urban Nationalist Feminist warriorwomen and make me seriously consider joining his crusade to save the country, my feelings for which *define* the word ambivalence, is more dangerous than the affable evil of Ronald Reagan or the fumbling fascism of George Bush.

Bill Clinton is dangerous because *he almost makes me forget to fuss.* He isn't scary because he excludes me. He's scary because he *doesn't.* He makes me feel like a citizen; a partner in the common good; a co-owner of shared heritage and future promise. He makes me feel like *an American* and even on election night, I am not too far gone to see the danger in any indulgence of *that* kind of longing to rewrite history, dismiss experience and pretend that Thomas Jefferson could have been *in love* with Sally Hemmings, even though he never freed her, and that Rodney King was the *exception* rather than the rule.

Even in my euphoria, I know *that* way lies the frustration of becoming part of a team that ultimately is still in the control of the usual suspects, and the madness of long, wasted evenings doing conversational missionary work at dinner parties where the only other black people present are summoned with a small silver bell at the hostess's right hand.

Better to remember the value of a critical eye, firmly fixed on the long view and the objectivity that only comes with being *an outsider by choice as well as historical imperative.* Better to repeat my mother's cautionary words as an election-eve mantra, hang the windows with wolfbane, and thank the goddess for making sure the other members of my household are asleep so I can have a good cry for the pleasure of patriotism denied and sing along as loud as I want to when they get to the chorus. After all, anybody who likes Fleetwood Mac can't be all bad, *can he?*

RECHANNELING
THE ENERGY

A few weeks ago, I found myself furiously writing another angry letter to the Mayor defending Sister Souljah's right as an African American Amazon Warrior to express herself as she saw fit without regard for the sensibilities of white, male presidential candidates and their supporters. I stopped in mid-rant to ask myself a critical question: *What was I so mad about?*

This was nothing new. The Mayor and I haven't seen eye-to-eye since he left the old neighborhood. But lately I was finding myself unable to read about him or listen to him without having a reaction that can only be described as out-of-proportion.

The kind of anger and disappointment I was feeling are only appropriate the *first* time the person in question deviates from whatever standard we have concocted for their public behaviors. On subsequent occasions, one must be able to simply add the most recent example of weirdness to the catalogue, analyzing and inspecting it for strategic reasons, but having no emotional reaction whatsoever.

I have achieved this level of objectivity when it comes to

the current crop of national political figures, but I continue to have a difficult time at the local level and when it comes to city hall, my expectations are always so high that I am inevitably disappointed.

But that's not this story. This is a story about rechanneling the energy. About achieving peace through understanding. About letting go and digging in; releasing the past and hurtling toward the future.

No one approaches the world without a point of view. A philosophy. Something that helps determine where we want to live and work and send our children to school. There are currently two major oppositional philosophies that determine the ways we as African Americans approach our lives in the U.S. Cities where we are the majority, including Atlanta. We can look at ourselves either as *African American Urban Integrationists* or as *African American Urban Nationalists.*

If you define yourself as what I am calling an *African American Urban Integrationist,* it means that you believe in both the desirability *and the possibility* of racial integration. In the face of overwhelming evidence to the contrary, you cling to the hope that racism can be completely eradicated.

You warm to Dr. King's vision of an America filled with color-blind children frolicking in the playgrounds of clean, well-lit, well-integrated public schools from which they emerge as perfect citizens devoid of racism, sexism and class prejudice, choosing of their own free will to live in neighborhoods that are economically and racially balanced, enjoying each other's cultures as if they were one's own, arguing spiritedly about the future of their beloved city.

It is a beautiful picture, as pictures go, although it has no relationship to the reality of urban American life. *African American Urban Integrationists* are working toward making this vision a reality.

Moving in another direction all together are what I call

African American Urban Nationalists. Drawing upon the wealth of experience and analysis left to us by Black Nationalists throughout our history, contemporary *African American Urban Nationalists* believe we must reclaim and revitalize our African American communities, which are where most of us live and work and fall in love and raise our children and grow old and die.

Being an *African American Urban Nationalist* doesn't mean calling for separatism. It means recognizing that *most of us are already separate*, by choice or by circumstance. For those who desire integrated living, there are many communities where that is available. But for those of us who want to live and work in African American environments, the choice should be presented as a blessing and a challenge, not a way to mark time until you can "get out of the ghetto" and as far away from other black folks as your line of credit can carry you.

There is no reason to assume that the *best* house, the *best* school, the *best* store, the *best* college, the *best* food are always going to be outside of our own communities. But that assumption is at the heart of the difference between *African American Urban Integrationists* and *African American Urban Nationalists.*

A couple of years ago as we were struggling to understand our role and responsibility in our community, my friend Zaron Burnett said, "From now on, let's think of Atlanta as a Third World nation." Somehow that clarified everything for me. A nation doesn't have to choose between begging and being defiant. A nation makes plans. A nation doesn't have to be mad because nobody else is taking care of things. *A nation takes care of itself.* Provides for the common defense. Makes sure everybody is clothed and fed and working at something for their own independence and the common good. A nation raises men to be brothers instead of predators, women to be sister-strong and mother-wise, and children to listen until they know enough to say something sensible.

I don't think we can go on any longer talking about crime control and economic development in a vacuum because if we do, we will never arrive at answers that do more than skim the surface. If we begin to define ourselves more clearly, we'll be able to identify each other more easily. Coalitions will form on the basis of common concerns and shared priorities. Things that used to be confusing will all become clear.

If someone says, "All the grocery stores in this black neighborhood are terrible. I'm moving my family to the suburbs," you'll know you're talking to an *African American Urban Integrationist*. If someone says, "All the grocery stores in this black neighborhood are terrible. I think I'll open one myself and fill it full of fresh vegetables and whole wheat bread and employees who live close enough to walk to work," you'll know you're talking to an *African American Urban Nationalist*.

I believe that until we agree on what we're really talking about, and why, we won't come any closer to figuring out what to do about it. I also believe it will be good for me to channel my civic-mindedness into more positive directions than writing mean letters to the Mayor. This way, with an understanding of his role as *African American Urban Integrationist* and mine as *African American Urban Nationalist Amazon,* we can salute each other from our respective battlements and let the games begin.

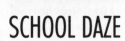

SCHOOL DAZE

The schools opened a couple of weeks ago with front-page news about a mini-riot between two warring factions of children who were said to be residents of two large public housing complexes that feed into the same school. The reason for the altercation, which apparently caught teachers and administrators by surprise, was some kind of rivalry about clothes, presumably the trendiest Starter jackets, or athlete-specific tennis shoes or X hats from Spike's Joint.

There were no white kids involved in this opening week fracas, which isn't surprising since the Atlanta Public School System is almost all black, just like the Atlanta School Board. These two black majorities *should* work together for the good of our black students since those entrusted with their care *should* have a clearer understanding of their needs and problems than people from some other community. (This is not to say anything against those Others. It is simply to point out that people tend to be more protective of their own children than of anyone else's.)

The problem is things aren't working out that way in the Atlanta Public Schools. Our kids consistently score at the bottom of national tests. Our teachers are underpaid and demoralized. The community is still largely uninvolved in deciding on overall direction and specific curriculum, and watching the school board meetings on TV sheds more heat than light even though some members seem to be sincere in their efforts to bring order amidst chaos.

This is very disheartening to someone like me who is a longtime proponent of community control of schools. *What is the problem?* While the situation is clearly a crisis of mammoth proportions, many of us seem to shy away from any real examination of the public schools. *Why?* After many years of considering this problem, I now have what I think is a credible explanation for our widespread avoidance.

We are afraid to look at our schools because somewhere deep in the recesses of our brains where racism does its most insidious work, *we are afraid that maybe white folks were right.* Maybe we can't have first-class schools without enough white kids to counteract the bad influence of our own children. Maybe we won't be able to excel in all-black schools, no matter what we do. Maybe, our self-doubt says softly, we can't make it without *them* being there to drag us kicking and screaming into perfect math SAT scores and scholarships that aren't based on our ability to play good football.

Well, those of you who have had that frightening thought can relax. The problem isn't lack of white kids. The problem is, as always, lack of *context.* We can't have a successful public education system without a clearly defined *context;* a world view; a philosophy; a way you want students to look at the world and a reason why. Incredible as it sounds, we have never developed that for our schools. When we think about it at all—and in America, we are always discouraged from thinking about context because it is easier to keep people oppressed when they are befuddled by the world around them—we pretend that there is one generic American point of view that we all—*all of us Americans*—agree should be taught in the public schools of this country.

Nothing could be further from the truth. There is nothing more politically charged and motivated than public education. This is the place where the State teaches its citizens how to think about themselves, about their country and about their future possibilities and responsibilities. And that is as it should be and it works fine as long as the State is a homogeneous group of people living together with a shared set of values and beliefs. The problem comes when you have a hodgepodge of very different people existing in increasingly uneasy proximity to each other such as we currently have in most American cities.

World view, philosophy and definitions of reality change from neighborhood to neighborhood, and even block to block, with breathtaking speed. A look at the responses to the Rodney King verdict makes this abundantly clear. While people in Beverly Hills were holding catered "Riot Parties" on their well-guarded rooftops, South Central L.A. was going up in flames of rage and despair.

Once we agree that context is important, we can begin to see why our schools are in crisis. We have not yet decided whether we are trying to train graduates to be *African American Urban Integrationists* or *African American Urban Nationalists*. The integrationists' dream is assumed to be not only the one we all agree on, but the only one *period*. We allow the schools to continue to use texts and teaching models that reflect an integrated, fair-minded, classless America that has never been more than a perverse fantasy for black people, poor people, other minorities and women, and is now simply our collective, recurring dream deferred.

Our children become increasingly frustrated and confused because we allow them to be fed a steady in-school diet of meaningless, unconnected information that is not grounded in the reality of their lives as young black people. Their completely legitimate, although largely unarticulated frustration over our inability to truthfully interpret the world makes them explode in seemingly inappropriate ways, but ways that are completely understandable once we consider how bizarre it must be to spend your days in classrooms where nobody tells you how to think about, and fight against, crack and AIDS and teenage pregnancy and racism and hunger because it wasn't in the generic syllabus that assumes the same reality for the suburbs as it does for public housing.

But there is an alternative. If our schools were being run by *African American Urban Nationalists,* the focus would be much clearer. Along with the required basic skills, we would be teaching our children a new set of three Rs—*reality, reason and revolution.*

Reality because fantasy enslaves. *Reason* because one of an oppressed person's most potent weapons is the ability to achieve clarity through reason. And *revolution* because we cannot help but want to teach our young people the necessity for wresting control from the existing order, which wants only to consign them to lives of poverty, drug addiction, brutality and despair. We cannot help but ground them in their specific blood-drenched history of struggle and resistance as we give them the skills, analysis, discipline and commitment to transform first themselves, and then their communities, and then their world.

And as an added bonus, in a school system devoted to producing *African American Urban Nationalists,* the question of life-and-death struggles over new Starter jackets or $100 tennis shoes will be moot because as part of our overall goal of achieving positive group identity, our children will wear uniforms, so they can stop worrying about who got what back-to-school clothes and concentrate on saving the race, which is, of course, the task at hand.

Isn't it?

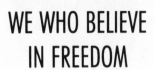

WE WHO BELIEVE
IN FREEDOM

Last month in the days following the Rodney King verdict, I turned on my TV one afternoon to catch up on things in L.A. and thought I had fallen into a time warp as scenes of students demonstrating in and around the campuses of the Atlanta University Center were flashed across the screen. As a graduate of Spelman College and a participant in many campus demonstrations, both as a Spelman student and before that as a Howard University student, scenes of marching, chanting students made me feel nostalgic and hopeful. It is my belief that conscious African American students ought to be in a constant state of rage *and* in a constant search for ways to channel that rage into freedom struggle.

I was pleased to see these students participating in a proud legacy of protest. Glad to see a now middle-aged Brother Mukasa still on the job as he was in 1969 when he came to speak at Yale while I was a student there for the summer and told me that I should probably sell my diamond engagement ring and buy some guns if I knew what was good for me and understood what America was really all about.

Watching those students marching downtown the night

the King verdict was announced, I remembered many demonstrations, from the takeover of the Howard University Administration Building to protest the war in Vietnam and
demand a redirection of the university's academic focus to
the intense debates at Harkness Hall between the Board
of Trustees at Morehouse College and a group of radical
black intellectuals—*teachers and students*—who had locked
them in to facilitate their reluctant participation in the discussion.

I remembered when The Institute of the Black World
opened on the corner of Chestnut and Beckwith Streets, and
hosted such revolutionary scholars as C.L.R. James, Vincent
Harding, Lerone Bennett and William Strickland who spent
hours engaged in discussions with passionate students who
quoted Nkrumah and Karl Marx and Sonia Sanchez all in the
same breath.

I remembered the hastily organized teach-in after the killing of black students during a protest at Jackson State where
participating faculty members made it clear to the protesting
students that the whole point of their being in college was to
learn enough to *do something* and so even in the midst of
protest they were expected to be reading and thinking and
discussing and strategizing. Everyone agreed that knowledge
was power.

But it quickly became clear to me that this was not 1967
or 1968 or 1971. These were students from a new generation
with an anger and a frustration specific to them. And they
were angry. At the verdict. At the police. At the violence. At
their own feelings of helplessness and betrayal and vulnerability. They threw bottles and rocks and dodged tear gas and
demanded meetings with high-level officials and ordered the
police to leave their campuses.

They taunted and turned tail. They demanded justice and
they looted a liquor store. They appeared before us in all their

contradictory young blackness, and when the media arrived and the cameras turned in their direction, and the microphones were pointed and poised, the question was asked, as they must have known it would be: *What do you want?*

And the silence was deafening. *What did they want?* Did they want to end the war in Vietnam? *It's over.* Did they want to demand black studies in their classrooms? *They can major in black studies if they want to do so.* Did they want an end to segregation in public facilities? *Done!* They were at a loss. They knew they were angry, but they weren't sure what they were angry about, other than the police coming on their campus and that couldn't be all it was since they were mad when the police got there.

What did they want? They wanted to be *included*. That's nothing to throw bottles about. City Hall is open every day. They wanted to be *considered*. No problem. Public meetings are announced in the paper every week so citizens can come and have their say. They wanted to *have a voice in things*. Great! Almost all of them are old enough to vote and to run for any office except president.

They wanted *black businesses* on their campuses. Sounds like a job for some business students who want to get some experience before they graduate and open their own businesses to help stimulate economic growth in the neighborhood and create jobs for their brothers and sisters.

So what's the problem? I felt like I was missing something. They were young and bright and literate and they lived in a community that needed all their skills desperately. They were being trained to be the leaders and the strategists and the builders and the dreamers at a time when their people had never needed them more. And they were miserable. Miserable and *confused*. Because nobody will tell them the truth.

On the contrary. We spend inordinate amounts of time lying to them, these who represent our best hope for whatever future we can squeeze out of this terrible place. We've raised them to think that they can give to the world the best that they have and the best will come running back to them, regardless of race and class and gender. We've convinced them that the world is waiting for smart, creative young black people who have only to complete their college educations and the jobs will be offered, the book contracts will be signed, the deals will be done and the paychecks will add up to forty thousand the first year out.

We've told them how different they are from their brothers and sisters living in misery just outside the gates surrounding their campuses. We've allowed them to use terms like *ghetto girl* and *project people* and not stopped long enough to explain to them that this is unacceptable language with which to describe members of your extended family.

We have ignored their angry rappers and their desperate movies and encouraged them to see themselves as *exceptions*. The ones who won't be ignored, brutalized, addicted, broken, beaten, raped, impregnated and abandoned. We've guided them into gilded cages and individual cocoons that seemed airless to them even as we extolled the virtues of that corporate office with a view or that new BMW or that Caribbean vacation.

And now, as Brother Malcolm would say, *the chickens have come home to roost.* The beating of Rodney King and the verdict ripped away the blindfold we tried so hard to tie across their eyes and they saw the America we had denied existed in all its brutal, videotaped glory. And they were surprised and scared and angry because we hadn't given them the tools to understand that for oppressed people, *freedom struggle is ongoing* and that the only real joy and happiness in life comes from passionate engagement with that collective struggle.

Confronting the Georgia Bureau of Investigation in the

middle of Fair Street is a hard way to learn a lesson, and as a friend asked me long distance, *didn't they know this was America?* But better late than never. They probably would have come along a lot faster and been a lot more articulate when CNN stuck a microphone in their faces if we'd talked to them a little longer and told them the truth a little more, no matter how terrible we thought it was. *Nothing is more terrible than not knowing.*

But all that's water under the bridge now. Now at least America has shown us all where we stand. The time for fantasies of individual salvation is past. We stand together or fall the same way. The police didn't ask Rodney King if he had graduated from Morehouse College before they cracked his skull.

So welcome to the battle, young brothers and sisters. *We've been waiting for you.*

PART FOUR

REASONS

TO

RIOT

AMERICAN PSYCHOS

S ometimes it is everywhere you look. The violence. The
  anger. The brutality. One time a weeping woman came to
my door at midnight because her husband was beating her up
on the street outside. And after we had helped her as best we
could and things settled down a little, my daughter said,
"They all find you, don't they?" And I said, "No, they don't
find me. There are just so many of them." So many of *us*.

*You're not going to write about that again, are you? You're not
going to start raving about that again, are you? You're not going
to bring up all that man/woman stuff again, are you? Can't you
give it a rest?*

Well, I tried. I really did. Ask anybody. I focused on the
war like a good African American. I refused to go see *Sleeping
with the Enemy*, even though I wish I'd thought of the title
instead of just living through it. I steered clear of battered
women's shelters and homeless women's shelters and the
welfare office. I curled up with mindless magazines instead of
Bell Hooks' new black feminist masterpiece and tried to convince myself things were getting better.

I reminded myself that "battered women's syndrome" is

now a legal term that allows a man's past brutality to be entered as evidence in a murder trial if a woman has killed her abuser. I re-read the clipping about the governor of Ohio freeing twenty-five women on the basis of this new defense. I sent a mental thank you to state representative "Able" Mable Thomas for being a courageous voice for women in the Georgia General Assembly. But like the song says, "There's always something there to remind me." In this case, two things: a book and a movie. *American Psycho* and *Silence of the Lambs*.

For those of you who don't know about these two contemporary horror stories, *American Psycho* is a novel by a young white male writer whose most famous book before this one was a chronicle of the life-styles of a group of young, white, wealthy cocaine users.

American Psycho, the author's newest offering, is the story of a youngish white male stockbroker-type who is so bored by his high-paying job, his aimless pleasure seeking and his beautifully tailored clothes that he tortures and kills a number of women, one black homeless man and one small child playing in Central Park. Each murder is described in horrifying detail, especially the sexual torture of the women, which is so graphically rendered and with such merciless unconcern, that I couldn't read them.

The book was rejected by one publisher after vigorous protests from women staffers, and got a lot of publicity since the rejection cost the publisher the $300,000 advance the writer was given, and the goodwill of First Amendment advocates and intellectuals around the country. Instantly picked up by another publisher, for another six-figure advance, the book was rushed into publication and is now available at your local bookstore.

That's one.

Silence of the Lambs is a movie based on the latest book by the author of several other novels, one of which introduces Hannibal Lechter, a fiend of a criminal who not only murders people but eats them. His nickname is, predictably, Hannibal the Cannibal. This character is the focal point of the movie, although there is another male character with the equally charming nickname of Buffalo Bill. He earned his moniker by not only murdering women but *skinning* them afterward. Something about wanting to make a suit out of female skin so that he could become a woman.

To say I was disturbed by the popularity of these two cultural offerings is an understatement. *I went berserk.* This went beyond woman hating into some new realm of madness that terrified me. I wanted outrage, I wanted protest. I wanted censorship, book burnings. I cheered the Los Angeles chapter of the National Organization for Women when they held press conferences against the book, and considered picketing my neighborhood movie house.

But somewhere in the midst of all that, I think it was while I was watching President Bush during the waning days of the war in the Persian Gulf, another thought occurred to me and I've changed my mind. Not about how dangerous it is to let this kind of hateful stuff pass itself off as *entertainment*. Not about how amazing it is that somebody is making all that money telling stories about men who torture and kill women, and black men and children. But about what the *correct* response is to such awfulness.

I used to think we should try to keep it off the page, off the screen, off the bookshop and video store shelves. I used to think reading it and seeing it only encouraged men to think violence against women was not only okay, but glamorous, seductive, exciting. I knew they sold every kind of violent pornography in the "adult" bookstores, but I thought we should take a stand when it tried to ooze into the popular culture, the local movie house, the mall bookstore.

I was wrong. We need to know. I think we should let *Them* let it all hang out. After all, *They* just started and finished a war and none of us seemed to have a clue as to what *They* were really thinking; what *Their* real motivations were. How *They* felt about things, even as *They* sent our children off to fight. And who are *They?*

They are the powerful white males who are still in charge of a lot of what goes on in this country. *They* are the powerful white males who still decide most of what gets printed and produced and distributed through the popular channels in every kind of media. *They* are the white male writers and directors who are simply translating the dreams and visions of their specific group into the artifacts of culture.

And it is as absurd for me to object to the horror of this wealthy, educated, white, American, male vision as it is for black men to object to the pervasive presence of male violence toward women in the work of black female authors. The objections are really beside the point. Whatever those of us outside the group feel about what we overhear as *They* are talking to each other, the fact of the matter is, *this is Their life*. And because we're all marooned here together, it's *our* life too.

I spend my life trying not to be afraid of the truth wherever I find it. If the cultural outpourings of wealthy white American men now reflect an anesthetized acceptance of violence toward women, black folks and children, I would do well to listen to the lessons I may find there. It might even be worthwhile to compare what they call "fiction" and "filmmaking" to the pages of the daily news.

It certainly wouldn't hurt to remember the words of advice Vito Corleone gave his son: *Keep your friends close and your enemies closer.*

And let the good times roll.

STRANGE BEDFELLOWS

I am not naive. I once worked at City Hall for two years so I know politics makes strange bedfellows. But I never expected to find myself in bed with 2 Live Crew. Figuratively speaking, of course, but even that is too close for comfort.

I didn't just discover 2 Live Crew. My daughter first brought them to my attention when she played me a bootleg tape of one of their first hits. The song was poorly recorded, but it didn't really matter since it consisted mostly of a group of rough male voices shouting the words "Hey! We want some pussy!" at the top of their lungs.

My daughter played the tape for me and giggled at my amazed reaction. I am, after all, the unshockable Bohemian mother, cooly able to transcend the creeping conservatism that is the curse of my how-can-we-be-forty-already generation. But this stuff was breathtaking in its bad taste; awesome in its anger; and throbbing with macho misogyny.

The other songs on the tape were equally offensive, although not quite as loud, including some completely vile interpretations of familiar childhood rhymes. "Why do you-all like this stuff?" I asked my daughter, who shrugged. "We just like the way it *sounds*," she said and giggled again.

And, I thought, remembering suddenly what it feels like to be so young almost everybody gets to tell you what to do and when to do it, they like it because it defies all the rules and drives their parents crazy. I advised my daughter not to play the tape for her father, who tends to be a bit more conservative about such matters, admonished her to be conscious of the sexist nature of the material and comforted myself with the thought that she'd probably outgrow the Crew at about the same time she discovers there are other things to spend money on besides designer tennis shoes.

The policeman who was on duty at my neighborhood record store didn't agree when my daughter and I approached the counter with a copy of the Crew's *As Nasty As They Wanna Be* several months later. The officer was aghast that my sweet-faced baby girl was being allowed to buy the tape. "Have you listened to this trash?" he said, giving me a firm enough look to make me reconsider the purchase. I nodded, paying quickly so we could make our escape before he arrested me for bad mothering. I knew he was only being protective of my child's impressionable ears, but I thought she was old enough to choose the music she listened to for her own amusement, even if I didn't find her choice particularly amusing.

And I *don't* find 2 Live Crew amusing. Musically, lyrically, philosophically or politically. From all I've been able to hear, read, see and surmise, Luther Campbell and Company are a nasty-mouthed group of crotch-grabbing woman-haters who not only couldn't leave a tender moment alone if they found one, but would probably feel compelled to club it to death with their penises.

As Nasty As They Wanna Be represents all the things that frighten and depress me about what many young brothers have become in these trying times. And Luther Campbell's self-righteous wrapping of himself in the blood-soaked hypocrisy of the American flag during the crisis over the banning of his record is due to American racism. But I can no longer allow myself the luxury of not taking a position on the question of 2 Live Crew. Silence, as the graffiti around town will tell you, equals death.

The thing that pushed me over the edge was the conviction last month of the Ft. Lauderdale record store owner who sold a copy of *As Nasty As They Wanna Be* to two undercover police officers. The owner (whose name, ironically, is *Freeman*) is black. His record store is in an all-black community. The members of 2 Live Crew are black. The jury, which had a majority of women, was all white. The verdict made the thirty-one-year-old Freeman the first American ever convicted on charges of selling an obscene recording.

News reports said that when the verdict was announced, Freeman, who faces up to a year in jail and a $1,000 fine, briefly lost control. He wept and then rose to denounce the jury as racist. "They don't know nothing about the god-damned ghetto!" he shouted. "The verdict does not reflect my community standards as a black man in Broward County!"

Which is, of course, the problem here. Decisions about what is obscene and what is not are made on the basis of agreed-upon community standards. It doesn't take a genius to know that the things a group of middle-aged, middle-class white women find unacceptable might not have much in common with what ticks off a group of working-class black folks who frequent the E-C Record Store.

2 Live Crew is no more ground-breaking in their nastiness than they are in the sampled mishmash they call their music. They didn't think up woman-hating, sexual violence or foul language. Their particular brand of swaggering machismo is no different from the sneering stupidity of comedian Andrew

Dice Clay and the heavy metal brutality of racist rocker Axel Rose. The difference is that these are young *black* men, the living, breathing, swaggering flesh of white America's worst nightmares. 2 Live Crew's angry thrusting of their collective verbal pelvises has struck a chord of white fear and guilt and anger that is now resonating through the culture with all the right-wing fanaticism that is the continuing legacy of the Reagan years.

And, unfortunately, all the hysteria has landed on the doorstep of Charles Freeman, whose personal freedom and family security are now in jeopardy because a jury of white people who have probably never even been in his neighborhood have decided to cut off the heads of the messengers who are bringing the terrible message of urban black male madness to the *Billboard* charts and into regular rotation on MTV.

Well, I don't need white America to protect me from young black men or to define obscenity for me. I don't think they're qualified. I think *racism* in all its deadly forms is more obscene than anything 2 Live Crew could come up with if they talked nasty for the next two hundred years. And until white America is prepared to do something about *that* obscenity, they can go fuck themselves.

ASSESSING ARSENIO

'm sure Arsenio Hall had been around awhile before I
discovered him. I think I had probably seen him a time or
two doing a few tension-packed TV moments of just-black-
enough-to-be-hip, stand-up comedy. I vaguely remember
him sitting around on one of those shows like "That's Incredible" but that was probably Byron Allen now that I think
about it, so it's neither here nor there to this story.

I only mention it because his face wasn't completely unfamiliar to me when he first showed up at Fox to replace Joan
Rivers, who had gone kamikaze on national TV, albeit late-
night TV.

Arsenio was as familiar as the boy who sat across the aisle
from me in math all the way through seventh grade. I think
it was the grin that stuck in my mind. Torturously tooth-
some, he smiled with the manic urgency of an up-and-
coming middle manager coming back late from lunch with
no good excuse and lipstick on his collar. There is remembered joy in it somewhere, but at the moment, the grin's
main goal is to diffuse any possible reprimand and reestablish
the kind of uneasy camaraderie that can only exist between

those who live to be loved and those who control the keys to the kingdom, or at the very least late night possession of the remote control.

The first night I saw him on Fox, he was grinning that grin like there was no tomorrow. He was talking fast and rolling those great, big innocent eyes and licking his lips and waving his hands and giggling and stroking his mustache and scanning the audience and listening for the laughs with such intensity that I was exhausted by the time he finished his monologue. Exhausted, but intrigued. He hadn't been boring, and he didn't seem the least bit winded by his efforts.

I don't remember what he was talking about specifically, but what I do remember is that he was talking like there weren't any white folks listening. Not that he was talking about race; he was just talking like a black person, which of course he is, which is why such a phenomenon shouldn't be surprising, but it really is when you consider how many times black people who make it to television are at such great pains to crossover and reassure their white audiences that they forget to touch base with their black ones.

All the nuances change. The jokes become more middle-of-the-road. The references have to be broad enough so that middle-aged, white viewers in Idaho can be amused at the same time that black teenagers in the Bronx are laughing. It is a delicate balance, and most of the time black performers fall off in the direction of white crossover and leave their black specificity behind.

We always understand, but we always miss the good old days when they were talking *to* us, *about* us. It's why we're so delighted when Bill Cosby calls Phylicia "Miss Thang" on "The Cosby Show" or Oprah calls her guests "girlfriend." It's why we still miss Richard Pryor, even all those bad movies later.

But Arsenio Hall is not Richard Pryor or Eddie Murphy,

although he owes a debt to both of them. He is something specific unto himself because he's working in television where the performers come into our living rooms and kitchens and bedrooms. We have to like them over the long haul, or they can't survive the scrutiny. I remember wondering whether or not Arsenio Hall was too "hot" for the coolest of the communications mediums.

But he surprised me. Once he got through with the monologue and sat down for the requisite celebrity interviews, he showed a remarkable facility for asking questions with absolute charm and enough candor to make the people actually try to answer. Whatever the reasons, I remember enjoying the show and actually finding him likable by the time they rolled the final credits.

Well, what happened after that is, as they say, history. He hit the big time, and now he's on five nights a week, up against Johnny Carson and Pat Sajak. I had to watch, and I will admit that at first I was worried. He looked tense and nervous. The famous grin seemed to be held in place by Superglue, and in spite of the intense hype leading up to the show, he seemed insecure, out of place, surprised to find himself standing there in the spotlight alone. Almost in self-defense, he seemed to be moving toward the middle of the road, guest rappers and barking audiences notwithstanding.

But then something strange happened. First, he apologized to his audience about a rape joke made the night before. Then he booked Angela Davis on the show talking about political prisoners and Communism and her new book, and she sounded great and looked wonderful. The following week, he had Jesse Jackson on, looking relaxed and happy, and Arsenio was the perfect combination of respect and excitement.

The upshot of all this is difficult to assess at this stage of the game, but it raises some interesting questions. Like, has a radical, black feminist infiltrated Arsenio's production staff in the booking department? Like, why does the audience who squeals for Bobby Brown applaud so enthusiastically for Angela Davis, other than the fact that they both had on leather pants?

It's too early to pose answers, and I'm too gun-shy to claim any kind of late-night victory, but I'm curious and I'm more optimistic than I have been since they took "Frank's Place" off the air. So, I guess it's not too early to wish Brother Arsenio well and tell him not to move too far to the middle of the road. Those of us who spend most of our time at the extremes have televisions too.

REASON TO RIOT

The continuing debate over Spike Lee's *Do the Right Thing*, has left me confused. The gist of several heavy, initial, critical blasts at the brother seems to be that the movie is so irresponsibly incendiary that it will cause black people to pour out of movie theaters across the country and, infused with a newly awakened sense of organized outrage, lash out violently at unprotected pizza parlors and unwary white folks out for an innocent evening stroll through the black community. One reviewer even went so far as to encourage presumably white New Yorkers to "pray" that the movie didn't play in their neighborhood.

Well, I saw the movie and I want any of you with worried white friends to let them know they can relax and focus their prayers on something more worthy of their efforts, like world peace or a cure for cancer.

Do the Right Thing is a lot of things, but a celluloid Molotov cocktail is not one of them. Far from it. Rather than peopling his film with nasty, unlikable, stereotypical white villains, Spike has created the all-too-likable, reassuringly human Sal. Rather than painting cardboard victims and righteously martyred heroes, Spike gives us black characters who are confused, undisciplined, loud, wrong, undirected, misdirected and directionless. They are as rambunctiously confused as they are painfully familiar, and while we cannot deny them, they are hardly the self-sacrificing role models whose untimely deaths are the stuff revolutions are made of.

They are, instead, achingly accurate reflections of the violent, valueless communities in which our children can grow up to tell their elders their pain is not valid and their advice is worthless. These are not warriors. These are walking wounded in biking pants and spotless Air Jordans and haircuts that make it clear you wouldn't understand the answer even if you could figure out how to frame the question. These are foul-mouthed activists without analysis, draped in Kente cloth and festooned with Africa medallions as if consciousness was a costume that could be purchased from a dreadlocked street vendor.

These are grown men with names like *Buggin' Out* and *Mookie* and *Sweet Dick Willie*, whose relationships with women seem to be largely a never-ending round of accusations of unreliability, unaccountability and general shakiness.

These are not the ones with the necessary gifts to inspire insurrection by word or deed. These are the ones we see all the time. Down the street. On the subway. In the house next door. Across the dinner table. They are angry with no idea why or what to do about it. They are frustrated and they remain completely confused. They are expectant but without hope or dreams. Spike has caught them in his camera's eye, warts and all, and presented them during the course of one long, hot day, and we cannot deny the sharpness of his focus, even though we'd like to *say it ain't so*. We cannot deny the legitimacy of Tina's angry dance during the film's opening credits any more than we can pretend not to notice Mookie's unflappable ambivalence, even when he is confronted by love, hate, children, violence and loss. We cannot fail to sympathize with Sal any more than we can help wondering how to appropriately mourn the senseless death of Radio Raheem—as unappealing a victim of police brutality as I have ever seen on the big screen!

Ultimately, what Spike has done is not create the kind of energy that demands destruction, but provided the kind of mirror that lets *us* take a long, hard look at *us*, hopefully as part of the process of change. And that kind of self-examination doesn't make you want to break something. It makes you want to *fix* it, I don't care what that white reviewer told his nervous neighbors.

So don't be scared of a riot. If you didn't run out and toss your garbage cans around when you heard about Howard Beach or Bensonhurst or the 1981 Klan lynching of Beulah Mae Donald's son in downtown Mobile, Alabama, you'll probably be able to keep a grip on yourself as you watch Sal's pizzeria burn to the ground.

Go see the movie. Ask your kids what they thought about it and listen when they try to tell you. Tell your friends to go see it and ask them what they saw and if it made them mad and what they think ya'll should do about it.

But if what you're really looking for is a good, solid reason to riot, forget about the movie altogether. Gather up some old newspapers and take a look at the activities of your Supreme Court for the last six months. Now *that* is a reason to riot!

WHOSE MALCOLM
IS IT?

S pike Lee is writing and directing a movie about the life of Malcolm X. The movie will star Denzel Washington in the title role, and will attempt to portray the complexity, commitment and contradictions of Malcolm's life within the space of three hours, give or take 15 minutes.

As seems to be the rule with Spike Lee movies and the marketing of them, there is already a serious controversy surrounding the production. A group of African Americans under the leadership of writer Amiri Baraka (formerly LeRoi Jones) are mad at Spike for having the *nerve* to try and make a movie about Malcolm.

According to published reports, they are afraid Spike will concentrate too heavily on Malcolm's early days as a pimp and hustler who went by the name Detroit Red. Mr. Baraka has been quoted as saying, "The life of Malcolm X is not another Spike Lee joint."

Well, I have a few thoughts on all of this confusion, which has already resulted in a rather bizarre public confrontation between Mr. Baraka and Mr. Lee on 125th Street several weeks ago, and a flurry of charges and countercharges appearing in publications as diverse as *Newsweek* magazine and *The Final Call*, but first I want to say a couple of things for the record.

I am a third-generation Black Nationalist. I say that with confidence in the correctness of my vision and humility at my good fortune. I also say it as a way of establishing that I have the necessary credentials to speak on Brother Malcolm without fear of censure from anybody, even African American intellectuals from New York. I *met* the man. I shook his hand and listened to him talking privately to my father about the struggle to which they had both dedicated their lives.

I was *present* when he delivered his historic "Message to the Grass Roots" at the King Solomon Baptist Church in my hometown of Detroit, Michigan, and I was proud to hear him quote my father's stirring introductory remarks several times during his speech. And I was *present* later when he spoke at Ford Auditorium the day after his house had been fire-bombed and he was no longer an invincible leader, but a shaken *father*, filled with concern for his wife and small daughters whose lives he knew were in danger as much as his own.

And I remember coming home from church that Sunday he was shot down, and drowning in the horror of it as I watched my family gather for whatever comfort numbers and memories can bring at such a moment. I remember feeling the shallowness of my pride in the new black hat I had been wearing and which I never wore again.

I know that I am among a very small group of people who are privileged to have *personal* memories of "our black and shining prince" and I fully intend to pass them down to my daughter and my grandchildren the way I will pass on the stories of their grandparents and their great-grandparents as far back as I can get before running into the insurmountable barrier of the slave ship.

But while I treasure these memories, I am not *precious* about them. I know that I am not the only one whose life he touched and changed in ways I cannot fully articulate even after all these years.

Zeke remembers fiddling with his small radio to get the broadcast from the Audubon Ballroom, only to hear through the static the announcement of the assassination. My late friend Dr. O. T. Hammonds remembered being a resident on duty at Harlem Hospital when they brought Malcolm into the emergency room and "everybody on the inside wanted him to die and everybody on the outside wanted him to live."

I remember an article Betty Shabazz wrote for *Essence* magazine several years ago in which she spoke for the first time of Malcolm as a romantic husband who left small presents hidden for her around the house when he had to be away, and who often called to sing to her long distance before she went to sleep at night. And all of these memories are as real as mine and as critical to a full understanding of what Malcolm was *to* us and *for* us as a people.

I also know that there are those who are too young to have any personal memories of Malcolm. People like my young friend Collier, who borrowed my collection of books by and about Malcolm to figure out what all the fuss was about. People like the swaggering young urban warriors who drape themselves in medallions of Malcolm as if his likeness was a talisman to ward off the evil spirits loosed by the Reagan years and nurtured by the Bush administration.

People like Public Enemy's Chuck D, whose angry reality raps brought Malcolm to the attention of a generation that gets most of its information from MTV. People like all those enterprising black entrepreneurs, who are busily silk screening T-shirts with Malcolm's face and words emblazoned across the front and selling them to the same crowd that favors tennis shoes by Bo Jackson and breakfast food by Michael Jordan.

And so be it. The more the merrier. Malcolm's memory is not a delicate hothouse flower that will be tarnished or destroyed by being touched by *us*—in all our ignorance, in all our political naivete, in all our incorrectness, and all our jive, double-talking, wouldn't-know-the-truth-if-it-hit-us-in-the-faceness.

Malcolm was, and is, stronger than that. Bigger than that. More complex and more wonderful and more terrible. No one of us can possibly get down the whole truth about Malcolm, and that is as it should be. His legacy lives in our *collective* memory, not in any one person's memories or analysis, no matter how well researched or well intentioned or politically "correct."

Malcolm doesn't need Amiri Baraka, in all his male chauvinist, born-again Marxist glory, to protect him from *us. Malcolm is us.* That's the beauty of his life and the importance of his growth and development and ultimate sacrifice.

Not that he was *better* than what we are, but that he was *exactly* what we are. And Spike can't diminish that and LeRoi can't claim rights to it and Warner Brothers Studios can't corrupt it no matter how many millions Spike is able to make them cough up for the project.

Because he was our black *shining prince* and he was a part of us, the best part, and whenever we say his name or wear his image on our T-shirts or buy his books, we honor Malcolm by keeping his presence alive in the cosmos so that his energy can continue to inspire us and challenge us and move us, finally, beyond the books and the movies and the pendants and the street-corner ego posturing into full-time participation in the freedom struggle for which he gave his life. Which is, of course, the only legacy worthy of Brother Malcolm.

"By any means necessary . . ."

DOWN WIT DEE

One of the things about getting older is that you begin to cut off certain areas of life that used to intrigue and amuse you.

For most of us, keeping up with the popular culture (which almost always means the cultural artifacts produced and consumed by people under the age of twenty-five) is one of the first things we let go.

We stop going to nightclubs because the music's too loud. We stop going to concerts because it's always such a hassle finding a place to park. We stop going to the movies because we can catch it on cable in a month or two anyway. And we stop listening to the Top 40 radio stations that play the same ten songs day and night because the rhymes and rhythms are geared more toward aggressively awakening teenage sexuality and less toward the intricacies of middle-aged monogamy.

The problem is that sometimes this lack of attention to the music that both shapes and reflects our children (those tied to us by *blood and/or community)* makes us miss important developments in their world, and by extension, our own.

It is in this spirit that I offer the story of Dee Barnes to those of you who might have missed it.

Dee Barnes is the hostess of a syndicated television show called "Pump It Up." Her show features videos and interviews with a variety of rap artists. During the taping of an interview, rapper Ice Cube, a former member of the group N.W.A. (Niggaz with Attitude), made several unkind remarks about his former band members.

Eager for controversy, Dee's producer overruled her objections, minimized her concern about the reaction of the notoriously volatile N.W.A. and aired the segment in its entirety.

The reaction was swift and immediate. A few days later, N.W.A. member Dr. Dre confronted Barnes at a press party. Uninterested in her frightened explanations, the six-foot, two-hundred-plus-pound Dr. Dre began to beat, kick and stomp Barnes in the middle of the crowded nightclub.

Fleeing in terror, Barnes made it to the ladies room, but Dr. Dre followed her, where, according to eyewitness reports, he beat her to the ground, stomped on her hands and finally had to be pulled off her.

As I write this, Dr. Dre has been convicted in criminal court for the assault and fined several thousand dollars. A civil case in which Barnes seeks damages from Dr. Dre is still pending.

Acknowledging the incident, N.W.A. member M.C. Ren said: "She shouldn't have did what she did. She knew the consequences before she did it." He concluded by saying that he thought it was all right for men to beat women "if they get out of line."

When I read this story, I was already frightened by what I was hearing from the "gangsta rappers." I was already concerned about the violent woman-hating that these rappers were recording. I was already horrified that N.W.A.'s latest effort, *Niggaz4Life*, had sold 900,000 copies in one week and contained songs like "To Kill A Hooker," and "One Less Bitch (I Gotta Worry About)."

Barnes' story only reconfirmed what I *already* believed about this branch of rappers so I simply filed it away in the part of my brain that is constantly trying to understand what it's like to be young and black and male in America. And that's probably where it would have stayed if I hadn't met the victim personally.

Dee Barnes is twenty years old. She is a tiny little black woman who stands no more than five feet tall, and probably doesn't weigh 100 pounds dripping wet.

When I met her, weeks after the attack had taken place, she was still scared of physical harm at the hands of N.W.A. members or fans. She had been followed on the street, threatened by telephone and accosted in restaurants by supporters of N.W.A.

When a friend and I dropped her off at the apartment where she was staying for a few days, she invited us in, and when we demurred because of the lateness of the hour, she confessed softly that she was afraid to stay alone since she wasn't sure who knew she was in New York for the weekend.

As I looked at her standing there, it suddenly hit me that she was all alone. That she had been abandoned not only by industry insiders to whom record sales are more cleansing than the blood of the Lamb, but by her conscious sisters and brothers of goodwill who move around in the wider cultural circles that exist *outside* the hip hop nation.

There had been no outcry from the black women writers (including me) who are old enough to be her mother and who have participated in vocal and sustained defenses of sisters Alice Walker, Ntozake Shange and Gloria Naylor when they were attacked by black men for creating "negative images."

There were no forums analyzing what happened to Dee

and what it means to the growth and development of women's voices in front of and behind the microphones of the hip hop world.

There were no petitions demanding the removal of N.W.A. CDs from our neighborhood record stores. There were no picket lines of solemn sisters outside the concert halls where Dr. Dre and company were performing. There were only a few asides in longer articles focusing on N.W.A.'s phenomenal sales figures and then, the silence.

And *why?* Because the noise of the world in which Dee Barnes lives and works—the world in which our teenage children go to school and fall in love and decide to have sex or not have sex—is so insistently loud and irritating to our thirty- or forty-plus years that we tune it out completely and hope it will just go away.

But what would we have done if Ishmael Reed had decided that writing an evil book like *Reckless Eyeballing* was not enough and had grabbed Alice Walker by her dreadlocks and thrown her to the floor in the middle of a reception at Charis Books?

What if Amiri Baraka had taken physical issue with Ntozake Shange's play *For Colored Girls* . . . and punched her out at a reading at the Oxford Bookstore? What if Gloria Naylor was shoved around during breakfast at Paschal's by large black men who were offended by *The Women of Brewster Place?*

We would not have put up with it, ignored it, or explained it away. We would have called each other and been indignant and sent letters and demanded apologies. We would have urged Alice to get a gun and learn how to use it. We would have volunteered to be Ntozake's bodyguards and made sure Gloria had enough sisters around her to head off any further incidents. At the very least, we would have extended the righteousness of our collective wrath and the tangible comfort of our sisterhood to the woman in question.

Which is what this is all about. I don't move around in circles where the men beat you up at a press party when you offend them, but I now know the risks of my sisters who do. And I also know that without the strength and sustained support of our public outrage, the sisters under attack will be isolated, abused and ultimately silenced.

So consider this another message from the front lines. And next time somebody tells you how much they like the intricate production values and "fat beats" on *Niggaz4Life*, you tell them you don't wanna hear it cuz you're down wit Dee. *(Yeah, you know me . . .)*

ROBIN & MIKE

I guess it was a *love* story. A love story for the eighties. A love story for that moment when, marooned out of time and space and place and mind, we arrive in the midst of America's final, frantic fall from grace.

A love story for the eighties: Robin and Mike. Coming to us every day and all the way via the pages of *Jet* and *People* and *The National Enquirer*, which boasts the largest circulation of any paper in America, *plus* the primo spot right in front of the cashier at the Big Star so you *have* to sneak and read it as you stand there waiting and woolgathering and trying not to look at a stranger's groceries any more than is necessary to keep her Captain Crunch away from your two-packs-for-one-price paper plates and you gotta look at *something* and all the classy magazines like *Essence* and *Cosmo* and *Woman's Day* and a poor, neglected copy of *Time* or *Newsweek* are all the way back at the end of the conveyor belt and it looks so tawdry to step back and pick one up just to flip through when everybody *knows* you're not going to buy it.

The National Enquirer loves Robin and Mike. More than Lisa Marie Presley's scientology or Elizabeth Taylor's bad back or Michael Jackson's newest eyes/nose/cheeks/chin and chimpanzee, does *The National Enquirer* love Robin and Mike. Why? Because they are *consistent*. Week after week, they manage to touch the tacky tabloid heart with true confessions and tearful denials; heartless villains and exotic primitives; private yachts and mansions fit for a king if he could just find a suitable queen. A warrior queen. An Amazon queen. A strong, free black woman with a clear eye, a noble chin, a perpetually straight back and a clarity of mind and spirit that would carry her far above the full-color front pages and the ruined BMW's crammed with Gucci luggage and all those broken dreams.

For a while, I thought I understood. See, once upon a time, I wanted a man who could carry me around like a baby, but know I wasn't one.

I wanted a man who could save me from myself and from himself and from all harm.

A man who would kiss me and miss me and kill for me.

So when I heard Robin Givens was gonna marry Mike Tyson, I thought I understood.

I wanted it to be a love story.

Where the heroine is true/blue.

And where the hero is true/blue/too.

I was *desperate* for a love story.

But now the King is prowling his expensive rooftops with no one to rub that big square head and lick that gold front tooth and say something straight and sweet and strong and smart because, remember, this is an *Amazon* queen we're fanaticizing about, not a purple-lidded media monarch who has now reconsidered and retreated and reneged and recanted and wept for all the world to see, confessing in public to crimes that should be exorcised in the private darkness of the heart.

But I was *desperate* for a love story so I tried to believe that she could really love him, and that he could really let her, and maybe they could save each other and we, in watching, might find some salvation too at the suggestion—just the *suggestion*, now!—that something good can still come around, even when you least expect it; even in our terribleness, marooned out of time and space and place and mind when some forgotten sins from long past lives have so angered the Goddess that she dropped us, defenseless and deranged, into the belly of the whale where even Jesse Jackson can't save us, even though I think he really tried.

But I was desperate for a love story, and besides the heavyweights have *always* loved the ladies. Golden girls in golden gowns, hanging on the arms of men so strong the protection is, at last, complete. Giants gentled by the power of love; humbled by women who could look into their faces and see beyond the power they were paid to exercise to the power that is priceless.

Joe Louis was crazy about Lena Horne, even though he said she had the nastiest mouth he had ever heard, but being as fine as she was, she probably had to do something to diffuse it, otherwise, nobody could've acted normal around her at all—least of all *Joe*, who one time even went so far as to pose in a yachting cap and navy blue blazer because they were going out on a boat, after all, and this was Lena Horne, after all, nasty mouth or not.

And Sugar Ray Robinson grinning at the side of Dinah Washington when she swept into The Rooster Tail or The Twenty Grand or Smalls Paradise and threw her head back and laughed the way women do when they are in love and don't care who knows it because the affair is just so *unforgettable* . . .

But those were different times. And this is not the love affair we're used to. This is a strange, new, eighties love. This is not the soft, dark beauty, finally, absolutely, unassailably safe in the arms of her champion. This is not the proud warrior finally allowed to compete in a ring where victory is so absolute that violence outside it is absurd. This is a strange new love between strange new creatures rising heartless and homeless and hungry-eyed from the madness of urban America in unlaced Adidas and bright red lip gloss and a weird, unfocused longing for something undefined and undefinable. This is angry, brain-dead love, slouching toward nowhere, holding onto nothing, recognizing only individual needs times two and private disappointments gone prime time public.

"It's been hell," she said, fluttering her mascaraed eyes. "It's been pure hell."

"I love my wife," he said, shrugging his massive shoulders, "I love my wife."

But I wanted a different kind of love story. I wanted a love story that didn't depend on a fleet of fancy cars and a New Jersey ghost mansion full of deceitful dimples and joyless French champagne.

I wanted a love story that picks you up from your death bed, carries you to the window and then dies in your arms.

I wanted a love story that stands outside your window in the rain, watching for your shadow against the light.

A love story that giggles in the dark and sighs in its sleep and smiles in the morning while it gathers you in.

A love story where the mother counsels the daughter in dreams and babies are born in concentric circles of strength and courage and strength and courage and strength and courage . . .

But not this time.

And not this place.

And not this public peeling off of skin.

It's too hard to watch it, wriggling against the ropes, demanding a recount, while the eye sees red where there is no red and the ear hears song where there has never been music until all that's left, down deep in the night, is the murder of the lovers and the dying of the light.

DRIVING MISS DAISY
CRAZY

The famous white guy poet who said that April is the cruelest month knew what he was talking about. It was a hard month for me, too. I thought at first it might have been income taxes. Or the post-tour let down after Zeke and I got back from a three-show blitz of the Northeast. But none of those seemed to really be reason enough for the continuing and often outspoken bad mood that dominated most of April. Finally, after several not-so-gentle suggestions from friends and loved ones, I separated myself from the group long enough to try and figure out what was up and why I was feeling so hostile and bewildered.

After several hours of mindless television viewing and random magazine perusal, I came upon a month-old copy of *USA Today* at the bottom of the stack of newspapers that regularly replicates itself in the corner of my living room. Suddenly, the answer hit me like a flash. My eyes fell upon the front-page story about the Academy Awards ceremony the night before. A picture of Jessica Tandy dominated the space and the headline gushed over the success of the film version of Alfred Uhry's Pulitzer Prize–winning play, *Driving*

Miss Daisy. The film won multiple awards, including Best Picture of 1989 and Best Actress for Jessica Tandy for her portrayal of the endearingly cantankerous Miss Daisy.

For those of you who don't keep up with such things, and I envy you the peace of mind that must come about as a result of the ability to distance yourself from the popular culture, *Driving Miss Daisy* tells the story of a twenty-five-year relationship between "Miss Daisy," a wealthy, old white woman from Atlanta, and "Hoke," her long-suffering, permanently bemused black chauffeur. Invariably described in reviews as "feisty" and "high spirited," Miss Daisy makes Hoke's life a living hell until his charm, understanding, patience and overall saintliness, coupled with her own fragility due to advancing years, make her finally see that Hoke is not just a black servant to be ordered around at will, but a complex human being who, as Miss Daisy says in what is said to be one of the film's most tender moments, is her "best friend."

As I sat there holding my month-old paper and reading the universal acclaim for *Miss Daisy*, I knew why I had been so evil. I'm tired of Miss Daisy. Sick and tired of her and her story and the fantasy she represents. I am tired of books and movies and plays written by white folks about the good old days when servants were patient, loyal, long-suffering and black. I am tired of stories told by white southerners of how much they admired the hard working black women who "practically raised" them and who they will call "Auntie So and So" without any idea of how offensive it is to my ears. I am tired of *the master* thinking he or she can possibly analyze, understand, represent fairly or stand in judgment—good or bad!—of the slave. It just won't wash, I don't care how beautiful the cinematography is.

The system of black southern servants grew directly out of the system of southern slavery and was based on the same belief in the inferiority of black folks and the superiority of whites ones. It was, and is, based on the same feeling that black folks are meant to be servants to white folks. And it is fueled by the insensitivity that lets wealthy white people think that allowing the cook to take home the leftovers after the dinner party, or have little Jenny Ann's old coat when she gets her new one, somehow makes up for all those long hours of hard work at very little pay, with probably no benefits or sick leave, and having to get up at five o'clock in the morning every day to catch those three buses that run early in the morning to be sure that all those invisible Aunties and silently smiling Hokes can get to work on time.

Driving Miss Daisy represents the most blatant kind of nostalgia in the face of a contemporary black reality that scares most white people to death. It puts forward the myth of the good master with as much self-righteous conviction as that other model of self-serving southern propaganda, *Gone With the Wind*. And toward the same end, to make themselves and any of us silly enough to *go for the doke* believe that those were kinder, gentler times when good people could see beyond each others' "quirks" and become friends across lines of color and caste and gender. It wasn't true then, and it isn't true now. But the truth is too scary, too volatile, too foul-mouthed and gold-chained and rap-musiced to please the arbiters of what is High Art and Real Culture.

It is no accident that *Driving Miss Daisy* and *Glory* (which shows black men fighting valiantly in a war that only resulted in their "freedom" as an afterthought) were highly praised and rewarded while the grittier and much-harder-to-look-at *Do the Right Thing*, established producer/writer/director Spike Lee's genius, documented African American urban rage in all its complex, constant, violent horribleness, and was almost completely ignored at the Oscars.

But that is, of course, to be expected. Miss Daisy couldn't possibly be expected to want to know more about Hoke than she could find out from seeing him starched and smiling at her kitchen door in the morning. It might be too disturbing. Too angry.

Long before I was born, my grandfather was a waiter on the trains that used to be a major form of American transportation. He told me once, years later, that he and the other waiters used to get tired of the wealthy white people who rode the trains and gave orders with the arrogance of those who are used to being served. But they had a way of getting back at these mean white folks, as my grandfather called them. Just before they presented that big juicy steak with the aplomb and style that people still speak of with awe, they would spit on it.

Take that, Miss Daisy.

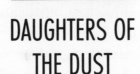

DAUGHTERS OF
THE DUST

I went to see Julie Dash's film, *Daughters of the Dust*, for the first time on a recent Thursday evening. Now, I had been missing *Daughters of the Dust* screenings for at least a year. I would either be leaving town the day before somebody screened it, or be arriving someplace where it had been screened the day before. It got to be funny as more and more women asked me if I had seen it, and I tried to explain that I almost had, but . . .

"You've got to see it," they would say with great intensity. "You've just got to see it."

Now, I always take recommendations like these seriously. That's the way people told me to read *Disappearing Acts* by Terry McMillan as soon as I could get my hands on it, or to go see Sweet Honey in the Rock next time they came to town, or to be sure and hook up with Johnnetta Cole when she came to town to become president of Spelman College.

These recommendations are always made by other black women, and the tone they reserve for these exchanges is so highly charged with sisterhood advice for survival and better living that I know it is foolhardy to disregard them. Sisterhood is powerful and my mother did not have a fool for a child.

I didn't know quite what to expect since nobody could really tell me what *Daughters of the Dust* was about. "It's beautiful," they would tell me. "It's like a dream." I could feel the skepticism on my face. "It's about us," they would say when I pressed them to be specific. "It's all about us."

I sometimes continued to press them but I knew what they meant. They meant that somehow Julie Dash had managed to write and direct and produce a film that showed African American women like we really are, instead of tossing us off as one stereotype or another. They meant we're going to be presented as fully rounded people, with the full complexity we know to be our birthright as human beings and our special legacy as African American women who have survived. They meant that Sister Julie had done on film what Toni Cade Bambara and Toni Morrison and Alice Walker and Paula Giddings had done in print.

Well, I had seen *Jungle Fever* and *Juice* and *Boyz N the Hood* and *Straight Out of Brooklyn* and enough rap videos to be tired of what *the boys* were telling us we looked like to them. I wanted to see what we looked like to us. As the lights went down, I sent a good vibe to Julie sitting in the crush of people up front in the crowded theater, and another to the lady with the fussy baby sitting too close for comfort, and turned my attention to *Daughters of the Dust*.

But wait a minute. I was immediately confused. *Who was talking? What were they talking about? What was the problem? Who was the little girl? Which ones were the newlyweds? Why was Eli so angry? Had somebody been raped?*

My brain was clicking frantically along at the rhythm of the *real* world—the *material* world—demanding the answers required in first semester journalism classes, but Sister Julie refused to indulge me. She was too busy putting together the amazing images on the screen before me—a woman in a billowing white veil standing in the prow of a small boat that is somehow steadied by her mysterious presence; an ancient woman squatting in the water with all her clothes on; a glass of water placed on a letter beneath the bed; a Muslim man at prayer by the water's edge; a book whose pages are gently rippled by the wind.

But who were these people and what were they talking about? I was confused, frustrated, restless. I wanted a road map, a clearly defined path that would use the same guideposts that I was used to depending on to navigate the shark-infested waters of modern-day, racist, sexist America. My brain was still racing along at urban hyperspeed and I wanted *Daughters* to hurry up and get on board.

That's what I *thought* I wanted, but Sister Julie was having none of it. She had placated and translated for enough money people and distributor people and second-guessing people to decide that when it finally got down to the individual moment in the darkness when each individual somebody has to look at the film and decide for herself if it makes any sense, that she, Julie Dash, was going to do just exactly as she pleased. And I understood all that, but I still *didn't understand/didn't understand/didn't understand.*

But then, just at the moment when I began to doubt the wisdom of my sisters whose urgings had lead me to the theater, a group of beautiful young black girlchildren appeared on the screen. They were playing on white sand at the edge of the blue Atlantic. They were laughing and tossing their braids and shaking their dreadlocks and switching their behinds in a game I remembered from my own girlhood on Detroit's west side: "Jump back, Sally, Sally, Sally, Jump back, Sally, all night long . . ."

Say what? "Here comes another one just like the other one . . ." and they collapsed in giggles as one of their number strutted herself down the middle of the line like she knew exactly how lovely she was, and wasn't it wonderful to be young and black and female and safe and dancing by the ocean?

And all of a sudden I understood. Not at a level that I can articulate in words, here or anywhere. But at the level that is quintessentially black and female, no matter who says what about it. At the level that is so exactly what I am that I don't even discuss it anymore since nobody gets a vote but me.

And my sisters. Because we know what is real and what is nonsense. Because we know we carry the genes of our mothers and our grandmothers and their grandmothers all the way back to where we were free women. Because we have what Martha Graham has called "blood memory" that transcends those things that can be put into words even by someone as passionate about words as I am—and must instead be understood in the marrow of the bones, the rhythm of the heart, the fullness of the womb.

That's the memory and the promise and the comfort and the strength and the courage and the truth of what I saw on the screen in front of me as Julie Dash's amazing film unfolded and I laughed and cried and clapped and hollered and felt stronger and wiser and more at peace because she had shown me the best part of myself right up there in living color and, to quote Sister Ntozake Shange, "I loved her fiercely."

So fiercely that I went back to see it again the next day with Sister Stephanie, and the next day by myself again, and the next weekend with my sisterstudents who stood on the sidewalk outside the theater with me while we shouted secrets at each other until the usher came out to tell us the people in the movie couldn't hear what Sister Julie had put together for them because we were making so much noise. And I wanted to say, *it's all the same dialogue if you just know how to listen!*

And watch. I've seen *Daughters* four times now and I wish

I could see it every day, just to remind me that I'm not crazy. Just to remind me of how beautiful we are. Just to help me remember how good it feels to be safe and free and happy enough to play girlchild games by the edge of the sea.

Art historians will tell you that when gallery owner/photographer/critic Alfred Stieglitz first saw the paintings of artist Georgia O'Keefe he exclaimed, "At last—a woman on paper!"

I know how he felt. Toni Cade Bambara says *Daughters of the Dust* is "the film we've been waiting for all our lives." And she's right, just like always. So if you haven't seen it, go see it. Twice. Take your sister. Or your daughter. Or your mother. Or all of them. Because it's about all of them. All of *us*. And, trust me, we never had it so good.

PART FIVE

STRANGER

IN

PARADISE

UNCLE ERNEST

In a family of honorable men, it is possible for a preadoles-
cent girlchild to have a crush. Fathers and brothers are out
of bounds. Too close. First cousins are usually against the
rules, but there have been many exceptions to this one that
worked out just fine. Second and third cousins, uncles and
uncles by marriage (under close supervision by the aunt in
question) are all acceptable crush objects for those years
when you still practice kissing on the back of your hand.

I was lucky. In my family, I had two crush-worthy third
cousins who exuded an air of rakishness and illegality when
they came over to talk to my stepfather and play backyard
badminton and tease us about still playing with dolls while
they were already spending their days in smoke filled rec
rooms plotting get rich quick schemes and getaway routes. I
admired them from the time I was eight until I went away to
college and didn't see them anymore, although I kept up with
their comings and going for a few years until they drifted out
of my life like summer romance at first frost.

But I said I was lucky. These cousins in themselves would
have been quite enough, but they didn't have to be. I also had

a crush-worthy uncle. Now I found all of my uncles interesting and attractive, but they never stopped talking long enough to have crushes on. My uncles were not the kind of men who enjoyed extended conversations with small nieces. Not that they didn't like us. They did. They just had more fun talking to each other. I understood. Along with my aunts, they remain the most consistently interesting group of people I have ever met. And I've been around the block a time or two with some serious contenders . . .

But that's not this story. This is a story about my Uncle Ernest. The first time I met him he had on a uniform. He was in the Navy and he was wearing dress whites. He also had a wonderful head of hair, gentle eyes and a mustache that drooped over the edges of his mouth like Emiliano Zapata's does in that photograph where he's sitting next to Pancho Villa looking much too dashing to be the serious revolutionary he was.

We were all gathering at my grandmother's house for Sunday dinner and my Aunt Barbara was there with her husband, or they might have just been engaged then, I don't remember. What I *do* remember is that when I was introduced, my Uncle Ernest extended his hand and greeted me with a courtliness that I had not encountered in any previous uncle, including my Uncle Winslow, who was unique in the fact that he was from across the river in Canada and when he said the alphabet he pronounced it "x, y, zed" instead of "x, y, zee," which was so amusing to me that I drove him crazy for several weeks so he would do it for me, starting from the beginning every time since that was part of the humor of it. He got tired of this game before I did and gratefully receded into the background uncles as quickly as he could.

But my Uncle Ernest was different. That uniform was part of it. None of the other uncles had been in the military. Several, in fact, had been conscientious objectors with the enthusiastic support of the family. Uncle Ernest was not only in the Navy. He had been wounded in the service of his country. I remember being acutely aware of the fact that his politics were very different from the other uncles and that they still seemed to like him, although the subject of the military was not a topic of conversation even though his uniform *glowed*.

When we were finally seated, my Uncle Ernest ended up next to me and when I reached up to pull out my chair, he bowed slightly and pulled it out for me. I was amazed and delighted. He smiled at me and then turned back to my Aunt Barbara, but it didn't matter. My crush was in full swing.

And it lasted, although my subsequent meetings with my Uncle Ernest were infrequent. His relationship with my Aunt Barbara wove its own complicated course through our family history and although I heard about him frequently from my first cousin, his only son, and others in my clan who have remained closer to home, I hadn't seen him since I graduated from high school, until last January.

I was in New York to promote the book my cousins had just published for me and they were stranded in the wilds of Pennsylvania with a van full of books and a dead battery. My uncle called the hotel where I had gone when I didn't see anybody at the airport to meet me and invited me to join him for lunch since the others wouldn't be in until several hours later. I accepted with pleasure, looking forward to seeing him again and for the chance to thank him for the bouquet of pink tea roses that had greeted me when I checked in. Something in me also knew it wasn't going to do anything for my confidence to spend my first few hours in New York alone. Too much time to wonder if I was really ready to do a New York media tour all by myself. I welcomed the distraction.

Uncle Ernest looked the same except that his hair and mustache were now completely white. He wasn't wearing a uniform, but a beautiful overcoat and a hat that he removed as soon as he saw me grinning at him across the lobby. We greeted each other across the years and I felt comfortable enough to tell him the truth when he asked me what kind of food I wanted. Italian, I said, and soon found myself in a small restaurant where the people greeted him by name and he asked them to bring a bottle when I requested a glass of champagne.

And we sat there and caught up and ate pasta and drank champagne and smiled a lot at his pride in his son and his new grandson and his curiosity about our book project. And the conversation proceeded at a rhythm that demanded nothing except a desire to relax and a willingness to tell the truth. And I heard myself talking easily as if we were old friends and suddenly New York didn't seem so intimidating and the idea that I might have something interesting to say didn't seem so farfetched.

As we got our coats to go, he looked at me and nodded with that same smile he had when he pulled my chair out all those years ago and let me glimpse what it was gonna feel like to be full grown, and said quietly, "You have turned out to be a very interesting woman." And I knew he had met enough of us to know what he was talking about. "Thank you," I said, blushing and feeling suddenly sentimental. "You're welcome," he said, as we stepped out into the snow.

And it was a good trip, and although we spoke on the phone before I left, I didn't see him again after that first day. And now I hear from my sister that he hasn't been feeling so good and that he and his wife have gone to spend some time with their son and his family. And I am sure that is the best medicine. So to their tender care, I simply want to add my best wishes for peace and strength and to send much love from a niece who didn't know a crush could last thirty years. But it can.

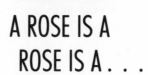

A ROSE IS A
ROSE IS A . . .

I t was Homecoming of my Sophomore year. I was walking
across the campus of Howard University with my boyfriend, a possessive pre-med student, who later revealed himself to be a womanhating thug, when I saw his older sister,
also a Howard student, coming toward us, arm in arm with
her boyfriend who was visiting for the big weekend.

My boyfriend's sister was a star. A deep brown beauty with
big dark eyes and a beautiful smile. She had come to college
with a U-Haul full of new clothes and missed being elected
homecoming queen only because the political winds had suddenly changed and we had to vote for the only candidate in
the race with an Afro. After all, it was 1967.

But that's not this story. This story is about definitions.
References. The calling of things by their proper names. I
was meeting my boyfriend's sister's boyfriend for the first
time. He was, of course, known to me by the 8x10 photograph she kept propped on her desk and the giggled quotes
she read from the passionate love letters he sent bi-weekly.
But this was my first time meeting him in the flesh and I
wanted to make a good impression. I wanted to be confident,

but cool; cute, but sophisticated; desired, but decorous.

My boyfriend greeted his sister with a brotherly kiss, draped his arm around my shoulders and offered this introduction: "This is Pearl, *my main squeeze.*"

It took years for me to appreciate his dilemma. *What to call the beloved in polite company? How to introduce a person who plays such an important role in your life, but whose relationship with you is primarily an intimate exchange that involves the rest of the world peripherally at best? How to make clear what needs to be clear without giving away too much, or too little?*

I never thought much about this problem when I was still a virgin. At that stage in the game, *boyfriend* covered the waterfront. It was a title that conferred special status; increased intimacy. Sexual exchange was not necessarily implied, but it was clear that if such an exchange was going to take place between the girlfriend and anybody, the *boyfriend* would be the one. After a certain period of time, which varied according to custom and personal taste, the boyfriend was allowed to lobby for sexual activity *unceasingly*, although he was never allowed to force the issue. That is called *rape.*

Boyfriend was workable up until I got engaged. At that point, my *boyfriend* became my *fiancé.* An even more exalted status and clearly indicating exclusive sexual activity within the socially acceptable convention of "soon to be marrieds."

Marriage makes everything clear. When you say "I'd like you to meet my husband" you define everything that needs to be defined in random social relationships between men and women. Sexual fidelity and economic interdependence are seen as components of a long-term relationship that all agree should be inviolate.

The problem comes when marriages don't last forever, to the absolute grave and beyond, and people have to introduce *new* people in their lives to *old* people in their lives and find a suitable shorthand to let everybody know what's happening. And to whom. *Boyfriend*, which was perfectly acceptable last time you were considering such questions, sounds a bit precious on women over the age of twenty-five. *Main squeeze* is out of the question. *Companion*, or *Life's Companion*, the terms favored by Sister Alice and others of the West Coast tribes is a little too serious sounding for me. *Longtime companion* reminds me of my friends who are dying of AIDS and makes me feel sad.

Lover, my introduction of choice based on hundreds of hours sitting alone in darkened theaters for afternoon showings of subtitled French movies, is a bit risqué for black Atlanta and *Sweet Thang*, the choice of the part of me that wants to sing like Chaka Khan when the moon is full, is a tad too personal for people who don't need to know *all* your business.

Well, the problem is, it's almost Valentine's Day and the cards demand that I call him *something*. I even tried *Sweetheart* under my breath at the Hallmark card store, but it sounded a little too old-fashioned for a man with dreadlocks to his waist and a personal history full of race men, highwaymen and full grown women.

Just like *boyfriend* and *husband* and *companion* and all those others sound too small, too still, too certain of things that can't be controlled, and shouldn't be, because then you can't appreciate them as much. Or hold them for as long. So I guess it doesn't matter what you say in introductions or how you define things for those who want to wish you well or offer their advice. A rose is a rose is a rose . . . *except of course, when it is an African Violet.*

STRANGER IN
PARADISE

A sister recently asked me how I am able to balance my Black Nationalist politics with my Black Feminist politics. I was a little surprised by the question, but I tried to explain that I don't see any conflict between the two positions. In fact, I don't think you can be a true Black Nationalist, dedicated to the freedom of Black people *without* being a feminist, black *people* being made up of both men and *women*, after all, and feminism being nothing more or less than a belief in the political, social and legal equality of women.

She accepted my response and I was happy to be able to help, but I wanted to caution her that the question of Nationalist or Feminist is only the tip of the iceberg and leads the truly thinking black woman inexorably toward more serious questions of balance and behavior. One of these questions confronted me on a recent vacation trip to Paradise with the object of my affections.

We spent a week in Negril, Jamaica, which is about as close to Paradise as I can stand, coming from the United States where the Paradise quotient for conscious African American women is depressingly low.

Here, we could be ourselves. Zeke became not an angry, exotic looking creature with "strange hair," but one of many dreadlocked brothers strolling through the town greeting each other with quiet murmurs of "irie" and "ya, mon!" Ron, the stateside video whiz, was so at home that it was clear this was his point of demarcation in some previous, sun-drenched life, and Mongo, my favorite "walking time bomb," laughed and joked easily with everyone from the airport security personnel to the beautiful girl who sat on his lap after the second day as if she could think of no more pleasant place to pass the morning. And eventually, I even found myself able to sit quietly under the biggest corn plant I have ever seen and let my mind *go walkabout*, focused on nothing except the sound of the afternoon showers and the memory of Zeke's hair floating out behind him during an early morning swim in the unbelievable blue of the Carib-bean ocean.

But it took me a minute. A *long* minute. *Why?* Because I have no experience with a lack of struggle, an absence of enemies and racial weirdness. I am unnerved by it. My heroes have been women like Ida B. Wells, crusading journalist and anti-lynching activist; Ruby Doris Robinson, driving force inside the Student Non-violent Coordinating Committee; Fannie Lou Hamer, civil rights activist and Mississippi Free-dom Democratic Party founder. I have studied hard to un-derstand the double jeopardy of being black and female in a place that is hostile to both and my vigilance within the borders of my home country is unceasing.

Even more to the point, perhaps, are the writers who stand beside my shoulder offering advice for correct living; Alice Walker and Maya Angelou and Sonia Sanchez and Ntozake Shange and the Tonis, Bambara and Morrison. These women have shown me by word and deed, how to dedicate my life to struggling for our collective freedom. What they have *not* shown me enough of is the correct mode of behavior for relaxing and recharging in an all-black Paradise.

Sister Alice's latest book teaches us that "resistance is the secret of joy," but what is there to resist in Paradise? What is there to protest and push against? And in the absence of the necessity for daily struggle, *what is a committed African American Amazon warrior to do?*

Where does the revolution fit into this house that has no walls, but only slatted wood and woven hemp and a porch upstairs where you can watch the full moon rise? What has the revolution got to do with this bed over which someone has hung a beaded half moon and the outdoor shower downstairs where you can stand naked in the sunshine surrounded by blossoming trees and cloudless sky? Is there no middle ground between the relentless woman warrior and the rock star's indolent girlfriend, lolling topless on the beach, nibbling papaya and sampling a spliff of the island's ganja harvest?

Realizing I was in danger of ruining a rare chunk of personal peace and tranquility, I cast about my brain desperately searching for a role model that could allow me to enjoy this all too brief moment in the sunshine. And I found one: *myself*. I am the one who has to enlarge our idea of ourselves to include time spent looking into the eyes of the people we love and seeing ourselves reflected back as we want to be, hope to be, could surely be in the absence of racism and sexism and rape and poverty and classism and homophobia and the Republican Party. I am the one who has to remind myself, and us, that the reason for fighting this hard is so that I can have more time to stand in the moonlight and drink rum with someone I not only would trust with my life on the battlefield, but who makes me laugh and understands the true beauty of a bed with a moon hanging over it.

So I relaxed into my few days of R&R behind the lines and

tried to remember that the ocean is still there being heart-breakingly blue even when I'm crying about the death of the misguided young brothers who regularly consecrate the streets of my neighborhood with their blood and trying to find a route from downtown to my house that doesn't make me a target for my brothers whose anger has made it impossible for them to see me as their sister and their comrade. And I made sure to write in my journal of the necessity for creating fully rounded women in *my work and in my life*. After all, even an African American Urban Nationalist Feminist Amazon Warrior needs a break every now and then.

IN MY SOLITUDE

I have been in love continuously since I was six years old. When I was in first grade, the six-year-old object of my affections had just moved to Detroit from Montgomery, Alabama. His wonderfully old-fashioned name was Turner Crooks. Now, maybe it was his shy southerness, in such sweet contrast to the more direct Detroit styles of my other classmates. Or maybe it was his closely cropped hair with the perfect part cut delicately into the left side. Or maybe it was the starched plaid shirts his mother sent him to school in every day. Or it might even have been something as mundane as the fact that "Crooks" followed "Cleage" in our alphabetized class roll, so Turner spent a good six hours of each day literally breathing down my neck. Whatever it was, he made my heart skip, my cheeks flush crimson and, for some inexplicable reason, my toes turn in.

This is a story about the years between ages six and thirty, when I spent a good portion of my every waking hour thinking obsessively and lovingly about one male or another. This is a story about that moment of realization that comes when you add up all the hours of your life and realize that you haven't allocated any time for your *self*. I realized this surprising fact when I was looking closely at how I spent my time, in the hope of squeezing out more of it to write (my passion and my livelihood). It seemed that I never had enough, and I couldn't figure out why. So I tried to examine my day and came up with the following percentages: Friends, 5; Family, 5; Child, 15; Work, 15; Maintenance, 10; Lover, 50.

I was appalled. As I looked at my list and tried to understand what it meant, I realized that there was no category for "Self." I had completely abandoned any organized attempts to spend time alone, enjoying and developing my own company, in favor of spending as much time as possible with the man who was closest to me. I had to admit that all the time I didn't spend working or raising my daughter or paying the gas bill was being gratefully, happily, excitedly given away to the man I loved.

I told myself that it wasn't true, that I was a conscious feminist who would never fall into such a trap. I told myself that I wasn't one of those women who becomes so man-centered that she blurs the line between *herself* and *himself*.

But is that all bad? I argued back to myself. A truly loving, liberated relationship is healthy, life-affirming, mutually beneficial and empowering to both parties. I reminded myself that my current relationships with men were (after many years of struggle) sane, affectionate, intelligent and supportive. I told myself that I could be alone whenever I wanted to, but that I didn't want to. I didn't need to. I've had enough time alone, I said to myself. Then another voice inside my head asked gently: When did you have enough? Which is when I realized that ever since I turned six and fell in love with Turner Crooks, the pride of Montgomery, Alabama, I had had almost none.

Starting with that first fall, I'd been in love and attentive in a way that had given me the ability to understand, interpret and appreciate the nuances of black male behavior in a way that delighted and inspired my men friends. Their reactions, in turn, rewarded and reaffirmed my worth in this distressingly male-dominated culture and convinced me, at a subconscious level, that listening to and understanding them was a far more critical and worthwhile undertaking than applying the same unblinking eye, attentive ear and generous heart to my own womanhood. But the question was, if I was looking at them and they were looking at them, *who was looking at me?*

As I thought about all of this, I realized that there were a number of things that were important to my inner strength and peace that I didn't do much of anymore. I listed ten right off the top of my head:

Things I Do Only When I'm Alone: (1) Write; (2) Listen to my Smokey Robinson records; (3) Buy flowers; (4) Make photo collages; (5) Think in the shower (or dream in the bathtub); (6) Read; (7) Sing; (8) Swim; (9) Meditate; (10) Plan ahead.

I was uncomfortably surprised by how many of these things that nurtured my creative life had been abandoned. I also realized that I had indulged in many of them only during the brief period following my divorce when I was too busy healing my emotional wounds to fall obsessively in love. I realized that I would have to validate the whole idea of solitude by choice and then figure out how to structure it. It was harder than I realized.

I was up against a culture that tells you the highest good is to find a man and spend every minute with him. I was up against women friends who say that letting a good man roam the Atlanta streets unattended, even for a few hours of solitude, is like dropping a lamb into a lion's den. I faced the insecurities that are the special purview of women turning forty. I was up against the guilt of not giving a lover my time and focus whenever he wanted them, a habit learned with the lesson of how to make conversation about sports. And, most persuasively, I was up against the sweet weapons at the disposal of loving black men who want to have your undivided attention. I feared that choosing to spend time regularly with myself was tantamount to taking a secret lover with unfamiliar habits and priorities. What was solitude anyway, I asked myself, and how was I supposed to get it? I decided to begin at the beginning.

One of my earliest memories is coming home from school to find my mother seated at the piano playing "Solitude," the Duke Ellington classic that Billie Holiday made her own. Now, my mother often played the piano and sang, but not like this. On these occasions she became somebody else entirely. She would close her eyes, throw back her head and sing with a fierce intensity and longing that I was still too young to understand.

She would still be wearing the same neat dress and sensible shoes she'd been teaching school in all day, as if it would take too long to change into more comfortable clothes. If she had stopped at the store, there would be grocery bags tossed on the kitchen table; ice cream and frozen orange juice being, at that moment, beside the point.

Although at that time my sister and I weren't really sure what the point was, we had sense enough to know that we should stay out of sight and sound until the moment passed. When my mother finished the song, she would sit quietly at the piano for a few minutes and then hang her coat in the living-room closet, and start on dinner.

My parents had been divorced less than a year at that time, and my personal theory concerning these passionate piano solos was that my mother secretly longed for a reconciliation with my father. When I asked her to confirm this theory years later, she laughed and shook her head. "Reconciliation? I was looking for someplace quiet to collect my thoughts," she said. *"That's* the solitude I was talking about!"

Solitude. Even the word sounds old-fashioned and wistful. It conjures up visions of large, empty rooms and lonely, reclusive people. Hardly a state anyone would yearn to be in, but hardly a definition that applies to solitude either.

Loneliness is to solitude what a beat-up old Volkswagen is to a new Rolls-Royce: You can live through the ride, but it doesn't do much for your peace of mind, which is what is at stake here. More than anything else, solitude is about achieving peace of mind, tranquility of spirit and clarity of thought. Loneliness is random; solitude is ritual. Loneliness is black coffee and late-night television; solitude is herb tea and soft music. Solitude, *quality solitude,* is an assertion of self-worth, because only in the stillness can we hear the truth of our own unique voices. Yet my associations with solitude have not always been so sweet. Solitude was something I backed into in self-defense when my other options seemed to run toward babbling at strangers on the telephone and weeping unexpectedly in the grocery store.

The end of my ten-year marriage found me in my own apartment. I was spending a lot of time alone, but my thoughts and spirits were more scattered than ever, and spending time by myself terrified me. Alone with my thoughts? Forget it! I became short-tempered and confused. My energy level fluctuated between manic and nonexistent. I was making decisions on my own for the first time, and I was uncertain about them. I was floundering and I knew it, but I couldn't find an organized way out of the chaos. Then one day I turned on the radio, and there was Billie Holiday, singing like a dream, and my mother's voice came back to me: ". . . someplace quiet to collect my thoughts. That's the solitude I was talking about . . ."

Suddenly it made sense to me. I recognized in me the same

yearning for solitude that I had heard in my mother's singing all those years ago. I wanted to know my own thoughts— away from all those absolutely-certain-about-everything male voices I knew. I wanted to hear myself singing. I began thinking about trying to structure some time alone with myself.

But how to begin? I knew structure was critical to the success of my quest; otherwise I'd use the time to sort the laundry or balance my checkbook. I decided to focus on creating a conducive environment.

Since the moon has always been connected with myths of female magic and power, the first day of the next full moon seemed like a good time to start. The time of day wasn't critical, but I knew I needed at least one uninterrupted hour. I made sure I had on hand things that were soothing and pleasurable—fragrant bath oils, fresh sheets on the bed, sweet incense and raspberry tea. When the appointed day and hour arrived, I dropped my daughter off with her father, unplugged my telephone, ran a hot bath, slid in up to my chin and waited.

I have to admit I felt kind of silly, hunched down in the water with the moon shining in my window, waiting for immediate and magical revelations to occur. But I made myself be still. I closed my eyes and let my thoughts roam freely.

And roam they did—to everything from my work, to my daughter, to my gentlemen friends, to my health, to my friends and back again. I didn't try to determine the right or wrong of anything that popped into my mind. I simply tried to be the same open, nonjudgmental ear for myself I try to be for those who are closest to me. And at the end of an hour, I was refreshed and energized in a way I hadn't been before. I was amazed, but still skeptical.

So the next day I tried it again, this time sitting in my

rocking chair just before the sun came up and my house came alive. I sat still for half an hour, and by the time I went to wake my daughter, I felt centered and ready for the day. I began to look forward to these times of solitude. I felt myself getting stronger and more peaceful as the weeks went by. Solitude became a regular part of my life. But what did I do with all this newfound, peaceful energy? I fell in love.

Suddenly the thought of spending quality time alone was replaced with a desire to be with the man I love. The benefits of solitude paled when stacked beside the excitement of an evening with him. Besides, I'd decided that all that contemplation, thought and listening to myself were only preparations for true companionship with A Significant Other. The healing effects of the last few months had lulled me into a false sense of security.

So I took my friend into my solitude hours and let him share the bath and smell the incense and replace my tea with a glass of chilled champagne, and it was wonderful. For a while. But then something started happening. His voice began to fuel my dreams. The beating of his heart became the rhythm I was seeking. And the *she*, who speaks so softly even loving male voices overpower her, began to slip away.

But I was not prepared to let her go. I had finally learned to depend on her, to listen to her, to trust her wisdom and her courage. I realized that the ear I wanted to bend with the particulars of my life was *my own*. The advice and counsel I needed most regularly were *my own*. I needed my own company, my own guidance and "someplace quiet to collect my thoughts" as much when I was happy as when I was sad, maybe even more.

So I assured my friend that this "solitude thing" was not a rejection of him, but a reclaiming and nurturing of a part of myself that was critical to everything I was or hoped to be. I closed the door upon myself, brewed another cup of tea, took a deep breath and sat down in my same old place to watch the moon rise. And the quiet became the stillness and the stillness became the peace and the peace became a path to a new way of life. I know my mother would understand.

MISSING YOU

February is a month that looms large in my life. Not because it is the month when the country we're marooned in celebrates the birth of two white male presidents we weren't allowed to vote for since we hadn't been declared people yet. And not because it is the month when we demand that attention be paid to *our* history (as if we could even begin to understand our history in 28 days out of 365!)

Not even because the most cursory look at the events that have happened in February might lead us to check the position of the stars, study the configurations of the planets and believe in black magic, *good and bad*, although I am the first to admit that February has something special about it.

Consider the possibilities of a month in which we celebrate the birth of Frederick Douglass, Eubie Blake, Leontyne Price, Langston Hughes and Marian Anderson, *and* the founding of Morehouse College.

What can we surmise about a month where we witnessed the assassination of Malcolm X in 1965 *and* Nelson Mandela's release from prison after twenty-seven years in 1990? What kind of energy is contained in a month that saw the first organized emigration of African Americans back to Africa from New York to Sierra Leone in 1820 *and* the beginning of the sit-in movement in Greensboro, North Carolina, in 1960?

But those aren't the reasons this month means a lot to me. I like February because it's the month my mother was born: February 12, 1922. It was always easy to remember her birthday because she shared it with Abraham Lincoln and we got a day off from school. She always said the holiday was really a celebration of *her* birthday, not his, and while we knew she was kidding, we really weren't. We figured she deserved it at *least* as much as he did.

The odd thing is that I can't remember the date she died. I used to feel guilty when people would ask me and I'd have to mumble something inconclusive. I could see how surprised they were that I clearly didn't remember such a painfully important date. But the date refuses to stay in my mind, no matter how many times I call my sister or check my journals.

After a while, I realized that my inability to remember it was not the result of carelessness or callousness. I realized that *how* and *when* she died was not the most important thing to me. The thing that mattered to me was the way she *lived*. I don't want to remember the false hope of medical miracles and the feigned concern of specialists.

What I want to remember are all the things that were the *essence* of her. The things that shaped my own ideas of what a black woman could and should be, to herself and to her family and to her people. The things that make me miss her more, not less, as the years go by. The things that still make me wake up wanting to tell her something; show her something; ask for her advice or her affection.

So February is mostly a personal celebration for me, although I always set aside enough time to say a prayer for

Malcolm, and thank the Goddess for Leontyne Price and W.E.B. DuBois. Mostly what I try to do is spend enough time by myself to conjure up her spirit to sustain me during these difficult days.

Mostly what I try to do is remember brushing and braiding her hair, or her brushing and braiding mine.

Mostly what I try to do is recall the warm ripeness of those impossibly red tomatoes she used to grow in her garden every summer.

Mostly what I try to do is play my *Madame Butterfly* records because she always liked to play Puccini, even when everybody else in our neighborhood (including me!) was worshipping Motown.

Mostly what I try to do is to remember how mad she was at me the one time I lied to her, and how seriously I took the promise I made to myself never to do it again.

Mostly what I try to remember is her pleasure in sitting around the kitchen talking and eating fried fish she'd caught and frozen the summer before.

Mostly I remember her delight in her grandchildren and the sound of her laughter that day we made a lopsided snow-woman by the edge of the lake and tied her apron on it.

Mostly I try to remember the cold floor under my feet that wonderful late-night moment when she woke me to come look at the deer nibbling delicately through the moonlit snow of the frozen front yard grass.

Because in the face of my memories, the date she died loses some of its power, even if it doesn't totally surrender. And I'm old enough now to understand that it's important to take what comfort you can in the face of The Big Questions about life and love and what happens after.

So I'll settle for remembering her laughter and sending her a happy birthday wish from her wild child, still struggling down here. And missing you . . .

TWINS

The thing about turning forty is that it makes you appreciate things differently. Not always more, although that is often the case—but always differently. You see things like time and space from another perspective. Mortality becomes a personal issue, rather than a philosophical one. Love has an added richness like a long-savored sweet. Children become a link to something bigger, more profound, and friends become precious in a way that can sneak up on you when you least expect it.

That's how I felt when my twin brother told me he was leaving town to take an offer he couldn't refuse from a big-time university in the wilds of North Carolina. He's not really my twin, but I was stunned by the emptiness of living in a city without his presence in it somewhere. Twins or not, we were friends-for-life, a rarified status that demands patience, a sense of humor and lots and lots of love.

On the day we met, in the midst of freshman-week madness at Howard University in 1966, I discovered two critical things about him. One, he had a serious crush on my new best friend, and two, we were born on the same day.

In the midst of that hectic week, there was something comforting about sharing a birthday with a stranger, and we relaxed immediately into an easy friendship that survived our mutual estrangement from my fair-weather friend, our first set of real college midterms and the student takeover of the university's administration building with a demand that the institution reevaluate its function in light of the reality of our lives as black people in America.

The flighty friend and the killer midterms were pretty standard collegiate stuff and we knew it, alternately comforting and challenging each other as the situation demanded. But the takeover of the "A" Building was in another category altogether. That was history and we were acutely aware we were participating in something more important than extended curfews and better food on the cafeteria menu.

The frantic organizing meetings brought us together more than the freshman boat ride or the traditional ceremonies had. My twin was a member of the leadership elite and his conversation was full of revolutionary strategies and workable options. I remember watching him arguing with a group of students on the steps of Frederick Douglass Hall and being both inspired and amused by his passionate defense of his position. I remember wondering where all that political energy was going to go once he finally got to be a doctor.

Because that was where his heart was. In medicine. The same love of black people that fired his radical passions at the campus gatherings that were a daily, sometimes hourly occurrence also fueled an intense commitment to mastering classes with intimidating names like microbiology and advanced organic chemistry. It was not unusual for him to exit a meeting just as things were heating up because he had a lab to go to or a paper to complete, but he was always back before the crucial vote or the final decision.

My twin was the first person I had known who was studying medicine because he wanted to heal people. In contrast to some of our more materialistic friends who saw medicine as the fastest route to big cars and fancy houses, he was always talking about accessible community health programs and better prenatal care and the importance of considering the complete environment in diagnosis and treatment of patients. Listening to him talk about medicine, I sometimes had that weird feeling you get when you see someone you love clearly through the prism of future possibilities and promises. I knew he was going to be a wonderful doctor, and he is, in spite of the long hours that wear him down and the babies that invariably decide to be born when he'd like a moment alone with his wife or the specter of ever-rising costs and never-enough resources to treat everybody who needs it.

We've tried to stay as close as we used to be, but it's hard no matter how much we promise each other. Sometimes it happens, in spite of our hectic schedules and other commitments. Like that afternoon when a mutual friend's unexpected death brought my twin to my door with thoughts of his own mortality, lending his visit the kind of self-conscious sweetness that makes a routine good-bye hug an awkward hedge against the uncertainty of good-byes.

Which is, I guess, what this is all about. Finding a graceful way to say good-bye to a friend whose essence even now eludes me when I want most to get it down on paper clearly enough to fix it in time and space and mind so that nothing can change it. But I don't think I'm any closer now than I was ten paragraphs ago. So, I guess the best thing to do is to take the villainous, fat man's advice to Humphrey Bogart at the end of *The Maltese Falcon* and realize that short farewells are the best ones. Good-bye, Ray, take care of yourself. You'll be missed more than you know. Where am I going to find another twin after all these years?

SITTING WITH
SARAH

M y friend is the kind of lawyer for whom the words "high-powered" were invented. Emerging from a family of strong-willed people to carve out her own niche and build a successful law firm, she makes complex decisions with an ease I used to find intimidating until I got to know her well enough to understand that in the circle she moves in, speed is a necessity, especially when you have the double distinction of being black and female. She who hesitates is lost, and all that good stuff.

Sacrificing on the personal side in order to ensure professional success, she learned to wheel and deal in the complicated real estate market of Southern California, helping her less-business-minded siblings secure their own futures while building on the family's holdings in a systematic way that impressed me even from a distance. She maintained a slightly bemused interest in my work and became a regular patron of the projects I am inevitably raising money for from wherever I can find it.

I appreciated her support, even though it surprised me at first. After all, we weren't alike in any of the ways you could see easily, and our relationship had admittedly had a rocky beginning. She holds the distinction of being one of the few people who has ever made me truly angry, but that's not this story. This is a story about Sarah.

It begins a couple of years ago when my friend took a look around and realized that something was missing. She was working hard, traveling widely, involving herself in the civic and political life of her hometown and overseeing the affairs of the family that expected nothing less of her. But she was looking hard at thirty-five, and if that doesn't make you reevaluate things, nothing will. Thirty is sobering enough in and of itself, but thirty-five is breathing down the neck of forty with such vehemence that any modifications have to be done quickly or all is lost and the specter of middle age is no longer something shadowy that waits in the wings, but something tangible that wakes up with little lines around its eyes and a vulnerability to the force of gravity that is nothing short of breathtaking.

In the midst of contemplating these inevitabilities, my friend realized that she wanted to have a child. She communicated the decision to me and I tried to be supportive, but I was too surprised to do much more than mumble something noncommittal and rush her off the phone, the fact that she was paying for the call notwithstanding.

I couldn't imagine her mothering. Nothing in my observations led me to believe she had either the stamina or the patience to deal with an infant, although she had a close, if highly charged, relationship with my daughter. I remembered enough about infants to know that being able to spend an afternoon at Saks with an articulate fifteen year old had nothing to do with getting up at 3 a.m. with a colicky baby. The fact that she would be a single mother, albeit a well-heeled single mother with a vast array of helpful resources close at hand, only added to my misgivings.

In addition to my concerns about her command of basic mothering skills, I was worried that she might be expecting more from the baby than any child can be expected to give. Although the afternoon soaps make it seem that the presence of a gurgling infant is a more certain panacea to empty lives and troubled marriages than a winning sweepstakes ticket, it has been my experience that small children rarely solve complex emotional problems. My friend's wistful desire to hear the pitter-patter of little feet toddling through her immaculate household when she arrived home exhausted at the end of her regular twelve-hour day seemed more than a little romantic to me. I wondered if she had, as my mother used to say, really "thought it through." I sent her a noncommittal note wishing her wisdom and clarity in her deliberations on the matter and hoped for the best.

Several months later, my friend came through town on a business trip. After exchanging the usual pleasantries, we sat down for some catch-up and she let me know that she was thinking even more seriously about the baby. She had decided to adopt, rather than pursue the other options available to independent women with the courage of their convictions. She was already involved in the process of interview and investigation that precedes any legal adoption, but she still wanted my opinion. Did I think it would be a good idea?

I heard myself sigh. I'm good at keeping my opinions to myself unless I am asked directly, at which point I think withholding your thoughts, if you have any, comes perilously close to lying. Understanding as I do that no friendship can survive without a commitment to truth, I opened my mouth to tell her that I thought it would be very difficult for her to absorb a baby into her demanding life; that raising a child alone was much harder than it looked and probably much harder than most single mothers will ever tell you; and that she might want to think about all this a little longer before making any firm commitments.

That's what I wanted to say. But I looked into her face and saw there her very real desire to bring a child into her life. A girl, she said, reassuring me that she in no way intended to take on the mysterious and challenging task of raising a male child alone. And suddenly all the practical considerations I was getting ready to encourage her to study seemed a little selfish and a little silly.

I was, after all, the same woman who had been tearing my hair out over what can be done to save the babies born to young, crack-addicted mothers, or the ones born under the death sentence of the AIDS virus, passed on by their often unsuspecting parents. I was the same woman who expressed a passionate belief that those of us with resources, conscious-ness and love to spare should consider adopting baby girls if we could see our way clear to do it without losing whatever tenuous hold on reality sustained us. I was the same woman who believed in the theory that if each free black woman would take responsibility for training one more, our numbers would increase slowly but surely until we might even be able to make some difference in how the world works.

So I congratulated my friend on her courage and told her I would help her in whatever way I could, whenever she needed it. She thanked me with a look of such relief and appreciation that I knew I had done the right thing. I was even more sure of it the weekend I first met Sarah, ten weeks old and already smiling at her new family. I was delighted to offer a couple of hours of free baby-sitting just to have some time alone to look at the beautiful Sarah and see if I could begin to think of her as my friend's little girl.

I didn't need to worry. She fussed for a few minutes before sighing deeply and falling asleep against my shoulder. I laid her down on my bed with enough pillows around her so that she couldn't have rolled off if she had wanted to and looked into her sleeping face. I could hear Charlie Parker playing "Dancing on the Ceiling" in the kitchen and smell the breakfast that Zeke had agreed to take over preparation of while I put the baby to sleep. I could see Sarah breathing peacefully and I think she even smiled in her sleep, although I'm sure the purists would try to convince me it was just gas. I don't think so. I think she was happy because someone had found her. Someone who loved her and wanted her and was prepared to try and raise her to be strong and free and independent, no matter what the world might think about such a proposition.

I looked at Sarah sleeping there and I admired my friend more than I ever had before. But then I felt myself getting sentimental, so I pulled the covers up around her and tiptoed out to breakfast, glad to be a part of such a sweet, new beginning. Welcome to the world, Sarah, and forgive me for doubting your new mother, even for a second. Even writers can be wrong sometimes.

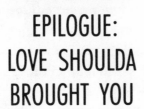

EPILOGUE:
LOVE SHOULDA
BROUGHT YOU

"If you cared anything for me
Then love woulda brought you to me last night."

Toni Braxon

I t's Friday, but I've given myself permission to sleep late without guilt and I am curled in the center of my bed enjoying that cozy netherworld between sleep and wide awake, congratulating myself on making it through 1992 and plotting my course through 1993. I hear her voice first. Loud and angry. Defiantly willing to wake up the neighbors so they can hear her wail of injustice and outrage.

"You hurt me," she says at a decibel level not usually heard at 7:30 in the morning. "Why you always gotta hurt me?"

I can hardly hear his answer. He is mumbling, his response completely without conviction. I get up reluctantly. They are just outside my bedroom window. She must be armed because he is backing away from her, careful to keep their old pickup truck between them.

"What you say?" she says, advancing on him. "I can't hear you. What you say?"

The pain in her voice is so resigned and complete, I want to jump back in the bed, pull the covers over my head, stick my fingers in my ears and try to remember giggling in the bathtub with Zeke last night, toasting the new year and looking forward to making love for the first time in 1993. I want to go back to sleep. *I don't want to hear this.*

His wife doesn't want to hear it either, but she has to hear it, this time and the next time and over and over and over again until she can't stand it anymore. And then she'll leave, if he hasn't already.

"How I hurt you?" he mumbles a little louder, still warily on the move.

"By bein' with another woman, that's how you hurt me," she says immediately. There is no question he can ask for which she does not have the definitive answer. She has been up all night asking and answering questions he hasn't even thought of yet. That's why she caught the bus as soon as it was light outside and came to confront him at his mother's house with a butcher knife in her jacket pocket and a simple question for which there is never a satisfactory answer.

"Why you always gotta hurt me?"

"Get the fuck outta my face," he says, his voice louder now, angry. I move to the bathroom window for a clearer view. *Should I call the police?* They are still circling the pickup. When she stops, he stops. The butcher knife is not in evidence from this angle, but it hangs over the exchange like Poe's pendulum. Zeke is already working downstairs so I know he hears them, too.

"I'm not gettin' outta your face," she says, moving a little faster. He turns and half walks, half runs in the other direction, making sure to keep the truck between them. "That is the one thing I'm not gonna do."

She stands looking at him across the truck bed. I hear her breathing and see his angry face, remembering suddenly that

I watched their backyard wedding from this window less then a year ago. It was an overcast day and they were racing the rain, trying to pretend they didn't notice the banks of clouds building up behind the house. The family had been cleaning up for days. Cutting grass, trimming shrubs, painting the back porch steps. The basement apartment in his mother's house that would be their first home together had been painstakingly renovated and was then filled by the groom's nervously tuxedo clad friends, already drunk and anxious to have the formalities over so they could get even drunker.

From this same window, I had a fairly unobstructed view of the back of the minister's head and the wedding couple's faces. I watched the bride exit the kitchen door in a short white dress that was already too tight for her. She draped her hand delicately over the beribboned bannister and descended slowly to the a capella strains of a large woman in a lavender dress and matching hat singing the Bill Withers arrangement of "Lean on Me." The groom exchanged a bored glance with his best man and sighed. The minister stood waiting in front of the freshly painted white trellis, now dripping with bright red plastic roses. The guests smiled hopefully, made the appropriate cooing noises and the proceedings got under way.

I remember wanting them to be happy. I remember thinking she looked a lot happier then he did. I remember her right after the service, surrounded by her squealing bridesmaids in their tight red dresses and high heeled shoes and wanting her to have a husband who would love and cherish her and greet the new year grateful to be in her arms. But *this* was that new year and she spent the night alone, at their new apartment, waiting for him *to want to come home.*

"Why you give her my money," she said softly. "Your *baby* money. I'm home by myself without no Pampers and you over here at your momma's house showin' out wit your girlfriend. If you wanted her, you shoulda thought about that before you put your thing up inside of me and gave me that baby."

This is too much for him and he lunges toward her suddenly, knocking the knife from her hand. She slaps at his face and they tussle for a moment below my window. He is breathing hard. "You better get out my face, I said. I'm not playin' with you."

She seems not to hear him although their faces are only inches apart. "You spent the Pamper money to buy her some Nikes," she says, equally breathless, and she hits at his chest and shoulders as he covers his face and backs away again.

I hear Zeke coming up the steps two at a time. "He's not hitting her," I say, knowing he is preparing to intervene and suddenly as worried about him as I am about this woman whose name I don't even know.

"He's about to," Zeke says, touching my shoulder reassuringly without breaking stride, tucking his pistol calmly into the waistband of his slacks. He heads back downstairs and I hear him open the garage door loudly. The man and his wife stop tussling and look toward the noise. Zeke busies himself with things on our side of the yard without acknowledging them a few feet away and clearly visible through winter bare bushes. The man looks at Zeke and then at his wife. Embarrassed, the woman returns the look and suddenly they become co-conspirators, walking casually to the other side of the yard together as if they had merely been engaged in a discussion of their pine trees. Barely out of earshot, they begin whispering at each other fiercely when a warning comes from the back window. *"Baby,"* says the disembodied female voice to her full grown son, "the police are here!"

Baby looks at his wife who puts her arm protectively around his waist. He hugs her shoulders and they walk together out to where two police cars sit waiting in their front yard. They are a temporarily united front, each working overtime to convince the weary officers that they were just talking and their presence there is not required. After a few minutes, the woman crosses the street to the bus stop and the man retreats to the basement apartment, slamming the door loudly behind him for the benefit of whichever neighbor called the police.

Once when a dazed and bleeding woman rang our doorbell at midnight after her husband had knocked her down on the street outside, my daughter said, "They always find you, don't they?" "No," I said. "There's so many of *them,* they find everybody. It's just that everybody won't open the door."

In the kitchen, I hear Zeke making coffee, putting on music, starting breakfast. I turn the shower on full force and as hot as I can stand it, close my eyes and step in, but the rushing of the water doesn't drown out the woman's question: *"Why you always gotta hurt me?"*

It's January 1, 1993, and I still don't know the answer. *But I'm working on it.*

ABOUT THE AUTHOR

Pearl Cleage is an Atlanta-based writer, performance artist, and award-winning playwright. She is the artistic director of Just Us Theater Company, editor of *Catalyst Magazine*, and a columnist for the *Atlanta Tribune*. She writes regularly for *Essence* and many other periodicals.

In 1990, Cleage published a collection of essays, *Mad at Miles: A Blackwoman's Guide to Truth*, that was based on her performance pieces and were the genesis for this book. Some of those pieces, including, "Mad at Miles," appear in *Deals with the Devil*.